John Eliot Bowen

The conflict of East and West in Egypt

John Eliot Bowen

The conflict of East and West in Egypt

ISBN/EAN: 9783337229757

Printed in Europe, USA, Canada, Australia, Japan

Cover: Foto ©Andreas Hilbeck / pixelio.de

More available books at **www.hansebooks.com**

THE
CONFLICT OF EAST AND WEST
IN
EGYPT

BY

JOHN ELIOT BOWEN, Ph.D.

NEW YORK & LONDON
G. P. PUTNAM'S SONS
The Knickerbocker Press
1887

This work is inscribed to the Faculty of the School of Political Science, Columbia College, to whom it was presented, in its original form, as a "dissertation in part fulfillment of the conditions necessary for the attainment of the degree of doctor of philosophy."

CONTENTS.

CHAPTER	PAGE
I—From Mehemet Ali to Ismail	1
II—Ismail's Ambitious Designs	18
III—The Road to Ruin	33
IV—Mehemet Tewfik, Khédive	67
V—Egypt for the Egyptians	91
VI—Arabi's Rebellion and the Reforms that Followed	113
VII—The Sûdan and the Mahdi	135
VIII—The Mission of Gordon—Operations in the Eastern Sûdan	151
IX—Gordon at Khartûm and the Government in London	163
X—Wolseley's Expedition.—Conclusion	177
Books and Periodicals Consulted	203

THE CONFLICT OF EAST AND WEST IN EGYPT.

I.

FROM MEHEMET ALI TO ISMAIL.

IT was not until the purchase of the Suez canal shares by Great Britain, in 1875, that the conflict to be described was waged with spirit. The influences and interests of the East and West, however, had clashed for many years. Long before the dawn of the nineteenth century the attention of England had been directed through Egypt to the far away Indian empire, that *El Dorado* that lured the British merchant-men to brave the storms of the southern seas. But the voyage around the Cape was a hazardous one and a long one ; and the growth of commerce demanded that the Eastern empire should be made more accessible. England knew, and the world knew, that the direct route to India lay through the land of the ancient Pharaohs. England thought the way through Egypt should be overland ; but France thought it should be by a canal that would one day connect the Mediterranean and the Red Seas.

France was interested in the valley of the Nile. She had put her foot there before England. The great Napoleon knew the value of Egypt. "By seizing and holding Egypt," he said, "I retain and command the destinies of the civilized world." And so, in 1798, he seized Egypt; but he did not hold it. The English, under Abercrombie, compelled the French to retire by the battle of Alexandria, in 1801. And now, for a short time, the influence of England was felt in Egypt. But it did not last long; for, after the accession of Mehemet Ali in 1805, Egypt was able to stand by herself. This event marks the starting-point from which it will be necessary to trace in brief the history and development of Egypt, in order to appreciate the government and condition of the country a decade ago, when England purchased the canal shares.

When the firman of the Sublime Porte made Mehemet Ali the governor of Egypt, in 1805, the country was in a state of feudalism. The pasha appointed by the Porte had been only the nominal ruler, the real government of the country being in the hands of the petty lords, or beys, known as the *memlûks*. They had deference neither for pasha nor for sultan. It is true that a small tribute was promised the Porte every time a new pasha was appointed;

but it was almost never paid. The governors had been many since the beginning of the century. "Indeed," says Mr. Patton, in his history of the Egyptian Revolution, "all the pashas that intervene between the French rule and that of Mehemet Ali are a will-o'-the wisp to the historian. A pasha of some sort flies before the eyes, but when we attempt to grasp him he is gone. . . . Thus successively rose and fell Mehemet Khûsuf Pasha, Tahir Pasha, Ali Pasha Gezairli, and Khurshid Pasha. Mehemet Ali alone stands out the distinct historical figure in the foreground." [1]

The obscure Albanian owed his elevation to the pashalic to his success, while a Turkish commander, in quelling the dissensions among the memlûk beys. Once at the head of the government, he set to work in earnest to deprive them of their power, knowing full well that his position as the sultan's pasha would be at best both insignificant and insecure, so long as these feudal lords played fast and loose with the resources of the land. Until 1811, therefore, Mehemet Ali devoted himself to the suppression of the memlûks. Against this grasping for power England entered a feeble protest; not indeed because she sympathized with Egyptian feudalism, but because she happened, at that time,

[1] A. A. Patton, F.R.G.S., A History of Egyptian Revolution to the Death of Mehemet Ali, vol. ii., p. 14.

to fall out with the Porte, and desired, therefore, to help the sultan's enemies. She even sent troops to Egypt and took possession of Alexandria. But the occupation was brief; for Mehemet Ali descended from Upper Egypt, where he had been administering such correction to the memlûks as few absolute monarchs ever dared employ, and, proclaiming himself the champion of Islamism, he forced the infidels to retire to Sicily. It now remained for the vigorous pasha to perform the two acts that consolidated his power throughout the valley of the Nile : the first was the revolutionary transfer to his own possession of the landed property of the entire country, and the second was the total extinction of the memlûks by massacre in the citadel of Cairo. The period of destruction was succeeded by one of development. The absolute ruler introduced modern military tactics and established a naval arsenal in Alexandria ; he built canals ; he introduced the culture of cotton, a product that was destined one day to become the source of enormous revenues ; he imported also indigo, forest trees, fruits, spices, *etc.*, for reproduction ; he founded medical and educational institutions ; he improved the police and rendered travel safe, so that now, for the first time, passengers and letters bound for India were conveyed with perfect safety through Egypt overland to Suez.

But Mehemet Ali was not content with these undertakings and improvements, important and difficult as they were ; he longed for greater power. He made war against the Wahabees of Arabia and he conquered the peoples of the Sûdan. And all the time he chafed under his subjection to the Porte. Finally he sent his warlike son, Ibrahim, to pick a quarrel in Syria ; and Ibrahim captured Acre and was soon fighting against the troops of his father's suzerain and carrying all before him. It seemed as if Mehemet Ali was about to become the sultan of Egypt and Syria.

This was in 1832, a time when England was keeping a very watchful and a very jealous eye on Russia, ready at any moment to claim a foothold in Turkey. England thought that Egypt, being *against* Turkey, must be *for* Russia. From self-interest England could not allow her "ancient ally" to remain between two such fires ; this Syrian flame must be quenched. England hesitated, however, to act, and in 1833 the Porte recognized the feudal sovereignty of Mehemet Ali over Egypt, Crete, Syria, and Adana, exacting only a small tribute. The peace did not last long, and in 1839 the Turks were again fleeing before the victorious Ibrahim. It seemed as if Asia Minor and Constantinople must soon succumb to him. But now England intervened with an energy that was wanting in 1832. Her fleet joined those of Turkey and Austria off the coast of Syria, and confronted by British commanders on land and sea the troops of Ibrahim were forced to yield. The hopes of Mehemet Ali were blasted. His son had been overcome by England and he had been duped by France. Thiers promised an assistance that was never rendered.

The war at an end, the Powers endeavored to negotiate a treaty. After the usual diplomatic formalities and delays it was finally agreed that Mehemet Ali should evacuate Syria, Arabia, and Candia, and should receive the hereditary government of Egypt, acknowledging the sultan as his suzerain. The terms of this agreement were embodied in a firman issued by the Sublime Porte in 1841.

Mehemet Ali was now an old man, and during the remainder of his life the influences of his youth and early manhood, as is usually the case with those who have witnessed and participated in great governmental and social revolutions, predominated over the progressive spirit of his most vigorous and potent years. He became more of a despot than ever; and his severity had few of its former excuses. He did, however, permit an association of British merchants to organize a transportation service to India, through Egypt, *via* Cairo and

Suez, by means of which communication with India was made in weeks instead of months.[1] In 1847 Mehemet Ali's intellect began to weaken, and within a year his dotage had so increased that his son Ibrahim was installed pasha of Egypt in his place. But Ibrahim's rule was cut short by death two months later, and in December of 1848 Abbas was invested with the pashalic. In the summer of 1849 Mehemet Ali died, spent in mind and body. A good idea of the character and work of this "Napoleon of Egypt," as he has so often been called, may be gathered from the following quotation from Mr. Patton's history :

There is much to be said in abatement of his merits. Although superior to a thirst for blood, from mere vengeance and resentment, and an easy pardoner of those who were no longer able to injure him, no compunction ever deterred him from removing the obstacles to his lawless ambition by fraud or force—most frequently by a compound of both. Nor was he able, with all his perseverance, to conquer his aboriginal want of education. Anxious to introduce European civilization into Egypt, he remained to the end of his life in utter ignorance of the economical principles upon which the prosperity of a state reposes. Greedy of the praise of Europeans, and, in the latter part of his career, anxious to count for something in the balance of military power, his allusions on this head showed

[1] William Holt Yates, M.D., The Modern History and Condition of Egypt, from 1801 to 1846.

to himself and to others the wide interval that separates the scientific organization of European military and political establishments from the Egyption imitations which cost him efforts so lengthened and persevering. But although unable to resist the dictation of any European power, he was—within Egypt—all-potent in establishing an order that had never existed before, so as to afford those facilities that have proved so valuable to the Indian transit. He found Egypt in anarchy: and long before he had terminated his career the journey from the Mediterranean to Nubia was as secure as that from London to Liverpool. He learned to read, and attempted to write, after he had attained his fortieth year; and when we add that the practical result of his efforts was to leave his family in the hereditary government of Egypt, Mehemet Ali must be admitted to have been, without exception, the most remarkable character in the modern history of the Ottoman Empire.[1]

Abbas Pasha succeeded Mehemet Ali. He pre ceded his uncle Said; for, by the then existing law of succession, the reins of government fell to the "eldest male of the blood of Mehemet Ali." Abbas possessed neither the warlike impetuosity of his father Ibrahim, nor the ambition of his grandfather Mehemet Ali. He did not look beyond the bounds of Egypt for territory to acquire or for customs to imitate. It was enough for him that he was a good Mohammedan; that the wheat and millet fields throughout the valley of the Nile yielded their

[1] Patton, vol. ii., pp. 17 and 19.

yearly increase ; that the fallahîn prospered and paid their taxes without the application of kûrbash and bastinado, and that there was peace among the people who acknowledged him their master. Though he did not court the favor of foreigners, he allowed an English company to begin the construction of a railway from Alexandria to Cairo, which was to be continued across the desert to Suez. But he himself undertook no great works, built no new canals, and did not even carry out the schemes and plans of his predecessors. Abbas has been called a bigot and a miser. He certainly was neither liberal in mind nor lavish with money.[1] It is not surpris-

[1] Abbas has had few defenders. Henry C. Kay, in *The Contemporary Review* for March, 1883, says of him : "It is not my purpose to attempt the impossible task of justifying every act of his government. But, as a matter of justice and a fact of history, it ought to be stated that he was probably, though without the advantage of European education, the most able and the most efficient administrator the country has seen since the death of Mehemet Ali. He has met with the misfortune of having his reputation sacrificed for political reasons. French influence was supreme and practically unchallenged throughout the reign of Mehemet Ali. Abbas Pasha, on his accession, manifested a disposition to seek some measure of support from England. He added an Englishman to the French officials employed at his Foreign Office. He set about the construction, under the superintendence of English engineers, of a railway destined to connect Alexandria with Suez, an undertaking until then successfully opposed by France. He, moreover, placed his son under the care of an English tutor. The consequences may easily be understood. But the curious part of the matter is, that English writers, by constant repetition, one after the other, have done more to propagate erroneous views of Abbas Pasha's reign than those of any other nation, the French probably included. It is not my object to defend Abbas Pasha's private character, further than by adding that the generality of the stories told about him rest upon no better foundation than the merest gossip."

ing, therefore, that at his death he left a large sum of ready money in the Egyptian treasury. Perhaps this was known to those who are said to have strangled him. At all events, the money and the government passed to Said in 1854.

Said Pasha was a very different man from his nephew Abbas. Their tastes, their habits, their dispositions, their lives, and, consequently, their governments, were diametrically opposite. In fact, Said was everything that his predecessor was not. Sociable, witty, extravagant, sensual, and fond of all the delights of life, he seemed rather the gay French courtier than the imperturbable Moslem ruler. He set up a court not unlike that of Louis XIV. He welcomed foreigners and entertained most lavishly. He forgot the sobriety enjoined by the Prophet, so that his dinners and his wines became famed for their richness and excellence. He accepted the suggestions of his foreign parasites, and hastened to adopt this scheme or that scheme, according as the whim of the hour or the persuasive agreeableness of the schemer might move him.

Among the foreigners attracted to Egypt at the beginning of Said's reign was a man of larger and nobler purpose than these grasping tricksters knew. Ferdinand de Lesseps had formed an early friendship with Said, while acting as diplomatic *attaché* in Egypt years before. At that time, also, he had conceived a plan destined to revolutionize the commerce of the world. It was not a new plan, however. The scheme of constructing a waterway between the Mediterranean and Red Seas had been suggested to all the great rulers of Egypt, the Pharaohs, the Persian, Greek, and Roman conquerors, and the Arab caliphs. Also, according to recent discoveries in the archives of Venice, it seems that the project of cutting the isthmus was considered by the mariners of the fifteenth century.[1] A canal between the two seas *via* the river Nile actually existed for an unknown period in the dynasties of the Pharaohs, and again for a period of more than four hundred years under the Romans, and lastly for a period of more than a century after the Arab conquest. But Mehemet Ali, though he had considered, had not favored the great canal scheme, and Ferdinand de Lesseps was obliged, therefore, to await a more opportune time for broaching his plan. He brooded over his idea of a waterway while England secured the construction of a railway.

With the accession, now, of his old friend Said, the cherished hopes of de Lesseps were kindled to expectation. Nor was he deceived in believing

[1] Robert Routledge, Discoveries and Inventions of the Nineteenth Century, p. 163.

that the opportune time had arrived. He went at once to Egypt and laid his plan before the viceroy. It was accepted by him on the 15th of November, 1854, in these words: "I am convinced. I accept your plan. We will talk about the means of its execution during the rest of the journey. [They were taking a Nile trip together.] Consider the matter settled. You may rely on me."[1]

The concession had no sooner been announced than English influence was brought to bear against the canal scheme. Mr. Bruce, the English consul in Egypt, told the viceroy that he was acting too hastily in the matter. At Constantinople Lord Stratford de Redcliffe threw obstacles in the way of the scheme, while in England the general attitude toward the canal was unfavorable, and even hostile. In January, 1855, the London *Times* declared against the proposed canal as an absolute impossibility. Lord Palmerston opposed the scheme from first to last. He held that the Porte must give its consent before the viceroy could allow the canal, forgetting that the English government had informed a former viceroy that he might construct a railway from Alexandria to Suez without the consent of his suzerain.

In February the sultan's council was on the point

[1] Ferdinand de Lesseps, The Suez Canal, p. 13.

of granting the necessary permission, when Lord Stratford interposed his influence to produce delay. His lordship urged that the railway ought to be enough without any canal. He hinted to the Porte that a canal might so increase the importance of Egypt that the child would break with its parental authority. An influence also was brought to bear upon the viceroy, but probably not of so intense a kind as de Lesseps imagined; for he wrote at the time: "He [the viceroy] is even threatened with the displeasure of England, whose fleets might attack him when the business on the Black Sea is ended."

The whole matter had by this time assumed an international importance, with France at the head of the nations who favored the canal, and with England leading the opposition. Lord Clarendon, in communication with the French government, said that Her Majesty foresaw inconvenience in leaving the matter to be decided between the sultan and his viceroy. He submitted the following objections to the scheme: 1. The canal is physically impossible. 2. The project would require a long time for completion; it would therefore retard the projected railway and injure Indian interests. 3. Her Majesty's ministers consider the scheme to be founded on an antagonistical policy on the part of France toward Egypt. The same objections and arguments were repeated by Lord Palmerston.[1]

All this time Said Pasha was harassed by doubts and fears; but at last, without receiving the authority of the Porte, and disregarding the attitude of England, he signed the final concession for the canal on January 5, 1856. It is said that he was influenced by the assurance that the canal would redound to his immortal honor and glory. Be that as it may, it is, in a measure, a monument to the generosity of the good-natured viceroy, whose name, at least, is perpetuated by the port at the Mediterranean terminus.

In 1858 de Lesseps launched his *Compagnie*

[1] The whole policy of opposition, as manifested by England, is thus humorously, but faithfully summed up by Mr. D. Mackenzie Wallace, in his Egypt and the Egyptian Question: "The consular representative of England does not approve the scheme, and warns his Highness against the insidious counsels of the plausible Frenchman. The cutting of a canal may be advantageous for humanity, or rather for that portion of humanity which happens to have a commercial fleet and seaports on the northern shores of the Mediterranean; but it would be ruinous for Egypt, because it would entirely destroy the lucrative transit trade, which might, on the contrary, be increased by continuing to Suez the Alexandria-Cairo railway. Then his Highness must remember that Lord Palmerston—terrible name in those days!—is opposed to the scheme, not from selfish motives, but because he fears that it is merely a first step to a French occupation, by which, of course, his Highness would be the principal loser. Lastly, there is the little matter of physical impossibility. The most competent English engineers—and his Highness is too well-informed a man not to know that English engineers are much more practical and trustworthy than French ones—have declared with one accord that the proposed canal, if ever made, will remain merely a dry ditch."—(P. 308.)

Universelle du Canal Maritime de Suez, with a capital of £8,000,000. More than half of this amount was subscribed for—the greater part being taken in France—and in 1860 Said took up the remainder, amounting to £3,500,000. De Lesseps began the work in the spring of 1859, although the consent of the Porte was not given until 1866.

The attitude of England toward the canal remained unfriendly. When the engineering question had been settled, and the feasibility of constructing the canal proved, the English began to assert that it could not be made to pay. The policy of opposition has been kept up even to the present day. As the question of the canal is to be dismissed now, and to be taken up again only incidentally, as in its financial bearings upon the relation of England to Egypt, it may be well to notice how England has persisted in what appears a jealous opposition toward the *Compagnie Universelle*. A single quotation will show how the London papers sought to bring the canal into discredit at a time when its success was still a matter of doubt:
"The Peninsular and Oriental Company's steamer 'Poonah,' with the Indian and China mails, which arrived at Southampton yesterday, experienced, while in the Suez canal, *a severe sand-storm, which commenced at sunrise and continued, more or less furious, until five in the afternoon.* During the

storm she laid [!] right across the canal powerless. *Tons of sand were thrown on the deck*, and the masts and gear were covered with a thick coating." [1]

Of late years the British ship-owners have come to wish for a canal of their own, and they are inclined to dispute the claim of the *Compagnie Universelle* that it has the sole right to control the canal question until the ninety-nine years of the concession are up. The British government, however, advised by the lord chancellor and the law officers of the crown, has been forced to declare that the company's claim is well grounded. It is to England's credit that the opinions of such men as R. T. Reid, Q. C., M. P., prevailed. This honorable gentleman said:

> The claim of M. de Lesseps and his company to equitable treatment is well known, and is more creditable to him than to the intelligence of our past rulers. The Suez canal is the work of his lifetime. He undertook it under circumstances of great discouragement. He completed it in spite of the disapproval of the British government. And when it has proved an immense success, and the navies of the world are reaping the benefit of his speculation, we are invited to find a flaw in his title, to chop logic as to the meaning of his concession, and to creep out of a difficulty which is a mere matter of pounds, shillings, and pence, by refining upon words in defiance of the intention. Such conduct would be unworthy of the British government.

[1] Quoted from the London papers of May 1, 1876, by Edward De Leon, in his The Khédive's Egypt, p. 36.

"... The canal is of enormous value to our shipping interests. It has saved us millions upon millions of pounds by halving or nearly halving the route to India, and greatly reducing the distance by water between us and our entire Eastern dominions. It is admittedly of the utmost political advantage to us with reference to India. This vast profit, infinitely exceeding anything gained by the canal company, has been acquired without risk of any kind to the British government, and, indeed, has been forced upon us against our will by the enterprise of M. de Lesseps. When the company who bore the brunt of the outlay ask for an infinitesimal part of the profit conferred upon England, and ask it in the form of dues stipulated before the outlay was incurred, we are invited to beat them down by the threat of a rival canal. This would not be creditable in an individual. It would be wholly unworthy of a great nation.'

And so the great nation decided.

But to return to Said Pasha. Having described his relations to the Suez canal, it only remains to record that he died in 1863. But, in passing, it must be noticed that a financial cloud, that was destined to blacken the Egyptian sky, and to let loose its bolts of distress and bankruptcy on the land of the Nile, was already discernible on the horizon. Said had exhausted the surplus accumulated by Abbas, and had left a debt of more than three millions sterling. How this was doubled, quadrupled, and doubled again under his successor, the sequel will show.

[1] *The Contemporary Review*, August, 1883.

II.

ISMAIL'S AMBITIOUS DESIGNS.

ISMAIL, the son of Ibrahim, the son of Mehemet Ali, succeeded Said. It is said that Abbas, long before, had been very jealous of him. He must, at least, have disliked him heartily; for the two men had nothing in common, and everything that the one shunned the other courted. While Abbas was ruling Egypt with a rigorous economy, Ismail sought the more congenial atmosphere of Paris. He obtained, in one capital and another, an intimate acquaintance with the civilization of the West, and stored his mind with all those pictures of European development that, though the result of centuries in Europe, he thought might be reproduced in Egypt within his lifetime. Having secured thus "a European education," Ismail returned to Egypt, after the accession of Said, and received from him a governmental portfolio. He seems to have had the entire confidence of the viceroy, for twice he acted as regent. He commanded, also, the year before Said's death, an expedition to the Sûdan. On his accession in 1863, therefore, Ismail was a man of experience—such experience as should have given him exceptional qualification for a ruler. But greater than all the wisdom, was the ambition that his observation had begotten.

It seemed as if Ismail's dreams of wealth and power were to be realized immediately upon his accession. Our Civil War was to furnish the means to this end. Europe had depended upon our Southern States for cotton, and when, by the war, the supply was cut off, there followed throughout Europe what has been called "a cotton famine." Especially in England the want threatened to become a great distress. The factories were closing, and legislators and economists were puzzled to find a way out of the danger. The shrewd Ismail, at this juncture, was not slow to perceive that the seed introduced into Egypt by his grandfather might bring him the coveted wealth, and he bent his entire energies to the production of cotton, borrowing money to buy the implements and tools, to secure the proper irrigation, and planning for work on a grander scale than the fellah at his shadûf had ever dreamed of. Ismail's success was greater than he could have expected in his most visionary moments. The soil of the Nile valley seemed admirably suited to the new industry, and every yield was enormous. The fellahin, the most conservative people under the sun, forsook their lentils, their millet, and their wheat, and hastened, in their humble way, to acquire wealth after the manner of their lord and ruler. And they prospered as their race has never been known to prosper from the time when their remote ancestors were the pyramid-builders of the Pharaohs, down to the present day. It was the Golden Age of modern Egypt. In three years the exports rose from four and a half millions to more than thirteen millions sterling. As is usually the case with those who enjoy unaccustomed and unexpected affluence, neither the viceroy, nor the great pashas, nor the lowly fellahin, made wise use of their prosperity. Their extravagances increased with their wealth. The viceroy thought that the influx of gold would be permanent, and he spent and wasted accordingly; the pashas believed that the vast estates that favoritism had bestowed upon them would continue to produce in luxuriance the white flower that was so easily convertible into yellow gold, and they lived their voluptuous life of Parisian and Oriental excess in their daira palaces; and the fellahin thought not and cared not, so long as their burdens were light and they could enjoy the sensual life that the Prophet Mohammed allowed them.

They all counted in vain. Our Civil War had come to an end, and the Southern states were again supplying the markets of Europe; the naturally fertile valley of the Nile, denied the necessary rotation of crops or the chemical fertilizers that the agricultural science of to-day substitutes, had been ruinously exhausted; and as a consequence the Golden Age was ended. All the extravagances reacted upon the fellahîn. The viceroy could not or would not contract his expenses, and, of necessity, he turned to the money-lenders and the taskmasters. The latter ground down the fellahîn to a life that was nothing more than existence. Exorbitant taxes were forced from them with the aid of the kûrbash, and their condition was more miserable than before their recent prosperity. At this time the cattle murrain made its appearance in the Nile valley, and the loss was overwhelming, and, of itself, sufficient to impoverish the people for a time. The Egyptian government, slow usually to give such assistance, was obliged to expend £5,000,000 to aid the suffering fellahîn. But, to offset the gift and in lieu of unpaid taxes, the land of the unfortunates was appropriated, not by the government, but by the viceroy himself. In the years that followed he became master, in this fraudulent manner, of one-fifth of the cultivable land of Egypt.

As the condition of the fellahîn grew worse, the

extravagances of Ismail seemed to increase. In 1866, at a time when he should have economized to the last degree, not only to relieve his country but to pay his own debts, which were already of a threatening size, Ismail, yielding, as ever, to his inordinate ambition, purchased the title and rank of *khédiv-el-misr* (king of Egypt) from the sultan. The firman that granted these honors and raised the limit of the Egyptian army from eighteen thousand to thirty thousand men, cost Egypt the increase from three hundred and seventy-six thousand to six hundred and seventy-five thousand pounds of yearly tribute to the Porte. From this time on the Khédive Ismail, through the most prodigal use of money-bribes and presents, secured a succession of firmans from the Porte. A firman of 1867 empowered him " to make laws for the internal government of Egypt, and to conclude conventions with foreign powers as to customs, duties, and the police, postal, and transit services. A firman of 1872 conceded to the khédive the power of contracting loans without the sultan's authorization "[1] —a power how used and abused!—and established the law of primogeniture in his family.[2] A firman

[1] John Westlake, Q.C., LL.D., England's Duty in Egypt, *The Contemporary Review*, December, 1882.
[2] This part of the firman, as it reads, " establishes the line of succession by order of primogeniture in Ismail's family—his eldest living brother, or this brother's eldest son, succeeding in case of failure of direct male issue,

of 1873, "which Ismail obtained by bribery at Constantinople on a more than ordinary scale, removed all limit from the numbers of his army, and empowered him to conclude conventions with foreign states concerning all internal and other affairs of Egypt in which foreigners might be concerned."[1] So much for Ismail's expensive relations with his suzerain. They had brought him, it is true, a power such as Mehemet Ali had dreamed of after the fall of Acre, but they had helped drag him deeper into the meshes of a financial snare, from which he was destined to escape only with the loss of all the powers he had inherited or so dearly purchased.

to the exclusion always of the female line. In the case of the heir being a minor (*i. e.*, under eighteen) on the khédive's death, he is at once to assume the vice-regal title under a council of regency. If, in his will, the late khédive have not nominated this council, the ministers of the interior, of war, of foreign affairs, of justice, the commander-in-chief of the army, the inspector-general of the provinces, in power at his death, will form the council of regency, and will elect a regent from their body. Should the votes be equally divided in favor of two names, the regency falls to the minister holding the more important department, who will govern with the council of his colleagues, when their powers have been confirmed at Constantinople by an imperial firman. The regent and the council of regency are immovable before the legal expiration of their powers, *i. e.*, before the majority of the khédive. Should one of the council die, the survivors have power to elect a successor. Should the regent die, the council will elect another from their body and a successor to the place he will leave vacant in the council." (Egypt under Ismail Pasha, edited by Blanchard Jerrold, pp. 71, 72.) This law reads well, and remains unchanged to-day. It did not provide, however, for such a forced abdication as occurred in 1879.

[1] Westlake, England's Duty in Egypt, *The Contemporary Review*, December, 1882.

Ismail's extravagances at home were equally enormous. When cotton was no longer recognized as king in the Nile valley, the khédive quickly proposed to substitute the culture of sugar. Not only did he proceed to cultivate the cane, but he planned to manufacture the sugar. For this purpose he built nineteen factories and refineries, and imported the best of machinery from Europe. This attempt to convert agricultural Egypt into a manufacturing country must always be regarded as the crowning farce of Ismail's reign. The country may be said to be absolutely without fuel; for there are no coal mines, and the tax-paying trees are too few and far too valuable to serve as fire-wood. With all his advanced ideas, the khédive seems not to have learned the first principles of political economy. Besides the building of the factories, a railroad was required to make them accessible. This was constructed from Cairo to Assiût at vast expense. Canals, also, were needed for the proper irrigation; and they, of course, involved another great outlay. But there was never any hesitancy on account of expense; and, the money being borrowed, the works were pushed ahead.

It would not be right, however, to attribute all the debts of Egypt, incurred during Ismail's reign, to his inordinate extravagance. The cattle murrain, for example, cost the government and people dear, as has been seen, but not through any fault of Ismail. In another matter the khédive laid a heavy burden on the government, but at the same time he won, and deservedly, the gratitude of his people and the applause of civilized nations. Said Pasha had promised to furnish the Suez canal company with a large amount of labor each year for the construction of the canal, and this labor was to be provided by the *corvée*, a system of forced service, in use as far back certainly as the age of the pyramid-builders. But it was disastrous to the agriculture of the country to have twenty thousand of the fellahin torn from their homes each month and forced to work on the canal. Ismail recognized this fact and abolished the *corvée*. It is generally admitted that he was influenced by humanitarian motives. And well he might have been! Our own most dreadful tales of slavery could be paralleled with the sufferings and tortures of those miserable mortals who were wrested from what little they had to make them happy in the fertile valley to endure the privations and almost certain death of that desert highway. Whatever the motive here, Ismail must always be credited with having performed a noble action. The canal company, deprived of the promised assistance, naturally demurred. This and a few other disputed questions were finally referred to the Emperor Napoleon for arbitration, and he awarded the company the somewhat exorbitant indemnity of £3,360,000. This was in 1864. In 1866 Egypt re-purchased for the sum of £400,000 a domain that had been sold to the canal company five years before for £74,000. It was a modest advance! Of course such extraordinary expenses as these necessitated new loans. All the loans that Ismail raised are themselves so extraordinary that their details must be noticed as well as the methods that the khédive employed in his endeavors to bear the burden of his obligations.

Before proceeding to the loans it will be well to form an idea of the revenue of Egypt under Ismail. To do this it will be necessary to consider the taxes somewhat in detail, although it is impossible, as Mr. Cave and Messrs. Goschen and Joubert found, to get perfectly accurate and trustworthy statistics on the subject, owing to the unsystematic and dishonest methods of a treasury system that was nothing more nor less than a hierarchy of swindlers, in which each officer got as much from the one below him and gave as little to the one above as was possible. What the amount of the taxes was before Ismail's time, one can only guess; but we may be sure that they never varied much from the utmost that kûrbash and extortion could raise.[1] The land tax, immediately after his accession, was increased by twenty-five per cent. This tax was again and again increased, until, in 1871, the famous *mûkabala*[2] was invented. This was a voluntary additional tax of fifty per cent. for six years, which, being paid, would free the land of the one assuming the self-imposed obligation from half the grain tax in perpetuity. The mûkabala was found to yield so readily to the demands of the moment—and Ismail lived in the present, borrowing no trouble from the thought of obligations to be met in the future—that it was *enforced* in 1876, and the period, at the end of which exemption should take place, was increased to twelve years. No tax ever met with such bitter denunciation as the mûkabala did from its inception to the day

---

[1] That the condition of the tax-payer has not changed much in three thousand years may be gathered from a papyrus in the British Museum, containing a part of the correspondence between Ameneman, the chief librarian of Rameses the Great, and the poet Pentaur. Ameneman writes: " Have you ever represented to yourself, in imagination, the estate of the rustic who tills the ground? Before he has put the sickle to his crop, the locusts have blasted part thereof; then come the rats and birds. If he is slack in housing his crops, the thieves are on him. The horse dies of weariness as it drags the wain. The tax-collector arrives; his agents are armed with clubs; he has negroes with him who carry whips of palm-branches. They all cry; 'Give us your grain!' and he has no way of avoiding their extortionate demands. Next, the wretch is caught, bound, and sent off to work, without wage, at the canals; his wife is taken and chained, his children are stripped and plundered." — Quoted by Blanchard Jerrold, Egypt Under Ismail Pasha, p. 164.

[2] *Mûkabala* = compensation.

of its abolition. It was bad for the payer and bad for the payee. "A ruinous financial device," says Blanchard Jerrold, "seeing that for a sum of in all less than twenty-seven million pounds, spread over a dozen years, is thence afterward surrendered for all time nearly two million five hundred thousand pounds of its [Egypt's] surest and most easily collected revenue."[1]

In order to form an idea of what the yearly revenue of Egypt was from 1870 to 1875, it is necessary to consult the reports that were made after that time; for up to 1875 there had been no attempt to estimate the revenue in detail. As the agricultural conditions did not vary much from year to year, the revenue during 1877, for example, would be approximately equal to the revenue during 1872 or 1873. This analogical reasoning is allowable, but not very satisfactory; for, unfortunately, even the *official* estimates of Europeans appointed for the purpose are found to vary greatly. The official estimate of Mr. Goschen, made in December, 1876, placed the year's revenue at £10,804,300. Mr. Cave's estimate for the same year was a little over ten and a half millions. Mr. Romaine gives the official revenue, month by month, for 1877, reaching a total of £9,350,274 for the year. The Cairene committee, in 1878, placed

[1] Egypt Under Ismail Pasha.

the total income of the khédive's government at about eleven and a half millions; but they considered this estimate low, and thought that, if it had been possible to count all revenues, the sum total would not have been less than thirteen millions sterling. This may readily be believed, if we may trust, approximately, the statement of Ismail Sadyk (the *mûffetish*, or "lord high treasurer" of the khédive, and one of the most notorious rascals that ever plundered a state and people), that he had raised by taxation in one year the sum of fifteen million pounds. But some estimates varied as widely in the other direction, and placed the revenue even as low as seven and a half millions. The extremes are far apart.

It will be interesting to separate one of the total estimates into its constituent parts; and for this purpose we may take the report of the Cairene committee. They placed

The land tax . . . . at	. .	£7,346,219
The date palm tax . . . "	. .	211,046
The house, shop, and mill taxes "	.	28,195
The poll tax [1] . . . "	.	630,204
Licenses and patents [2]	. .	798,253

[1] This tax was divided into three classes: viz., 40, 30, and 15 piasters. The collectors, however, were instructed to produce an average of 30 piasters ($1.50) a head.

[2] These were imposed on all servants, operatives, tradesmen, and merchants.

MISCELLANEOUS TAXES.

1. Succession or transfer duties on legacies, mortgages, etc. £103,685
2. Stamp tax (no statistics).
3. Salt tax [1] 400,000
4. *Octroi* and road duties on produce, fodder, and building materials [2] 328,872
5. Customs 639,000
6. Navigation dues 110,185
7. Duties on fisheries 33,548
8. Law taxes 44,392
9. Tobacco tax 106,777
10. Tax on cattle sales 45,402
11. Sheep slaughtered for food 14,769
12. Animal tax 8,479
13. Stamp tax on manufactured goods . . 18,000
14. Payments of railways into Public Debt Department 602,990

Total . . . [3]£11,470,016

From the foregoing notes and figures it will be seen that it is almost impossible to exaggerate the extortionate character of taxation in Egypt a dec-

[1] Nine piasters imposed on every man, woman, and child over seven years of age.

[2] This figure the committee considered small, since irregular government expenses were taken out of the *octroi* receipts, as, for example, the salaries of a *corps de ballet!* When, later, Egypt came under European control, the comptroller general encountered much opposition by his refusal to pay such salaries from such a fund.

[3] Other taxes, as on fire engines, ferries, jewelry, burials, marriages, tolls on bridges, and exemption from military service, were not counted, owing to absence of trustworthy statistics.

ade ago. But it should be noticed in passing that the land of the natives only was taxed; by a monstrous injustice—an injustice that continues to the present day, though there is just now a prospect of its being remedied—the European property-holders have never paid so much as a brass farthing into the state treasury on the land they have held.

Whether, now, we place the yearly revenue at the lowest estimate, seven millions sterling, or at the highest, thirteen millions, or midway between the two, the fact always remains the same—that Ismail was unable to live within his income. With the same revenue Mehemet Ali would have made Egypt independent of Turkey, and himself the champion of all Islam. Even the gay Said would have been at a loss for ways to squander such undreamed-of means. But with Ismail it was different. As we have seen, he could not forget the splendors of European courts, nor cease to envy the civilization of western countries; nor could he contract the extravagances he had learned in the days when "cotton was king" in Egypt. If he could not live and flourish and build and spend on the strength of his internal resources, he knew that there were bankers and money-lenders in Europe who would consider the yearly overflow of the Nile the best of security. The story of his transactions with these unbelievers forms the most important chapter in the modern history of Egypt; but the story is devoid of romance; it is as bold and bald and true as the working of a natural law. For the state, as for the individual, when debts are contracted to pay other debts, when further sums are borrowed to pay those, and when this system of discharging obligations is continued, the end is ruin. In the case of Egypt, the ever impending ruin has been long averted, owing as much (or more) to the political importance of the country as to its inherent wealth; but the burning question of that land to-day is the question of finance; for the debts that are due to the follies of Ismail still stand, an unmanageable burden. And this is how the first khédive brought about the financial disaster, and his own downfall.

III.

THE ROAD TO RUIN.

IT will be remembered that Said left a debt of about three millions sterling. To be exact, he had effected in 1862 a seven per cent. loan in the European market of £3,292,800.[1] Of course he

[1] For facts and figures I depend chiefly upon J. C. McCoan's Egypt As It Is, and upon Mr. Cave's Report of 1876, from which the following concise table is taken:

LOAN OF	To be paid off in	Nominal amount of loan, but real debt of state.	Charge on nominal amount.			Amount realized.	Real charges on amount realized.		
			Int.	Sinking fund.	Total.		Int.	Sinking fund.	Total.
		£	pr. c.	pr. c.	pr. c.	£	pr. c.	pr. c.	pr. c.
1862	1892	3,292,800	7	1	8	(a)	...	...	...
1864	1879	5,704,200	7	3.87	10.87	4,864,063	8.2	4.5	12.7
1866	1874	3,000,000	7	...	...	2,640,000 (b)	8	18.9	26.9
1868	1898	11,890,000	7	1	8	7,193,334	11.56	1.68	13.24
1873	1903	32,000,000	7	1	8	20,740,077	10.8	1.56	12.36
		55,887,000				35,437,474			
Daira taken over by the state.									
1866	1881	3,000,000	9	3.27	12.27	3,000,000 (c)	...	...	12.27
1867	1881	2,080,000	9	3.4	12.4	2,080,000 (c)	...	...	17.04
Daira loan of Ismail.						5,080,000			
1870	1890	7,142,860	7	2.35	9.35	5,000,000	10	3.36	13.36

(a) No particulars of amount realized.
(b) Railway loan repaid by six annual payments of £500,000, equivalent to a sinking fund of 18.9 per cent.
(c) No particulars of amounts realized, but probably the whole.

did not receive this amount entire, for the commission rate of issue, *etc.*, reduced the sum paid into the Egyptian treasury to £2,500,000. But this loan did not prevent Said from leaving a further legacy of liabilities, which necessitated a second loan within a year after his death. The amount of this one, which was raised in England, was £5,704,200. It yielded to the treasury only £4,864,063. And still the indebtedness was not covered. Up to this time the financial troubles had come through no fault of Ismail's. But in 1866 he had begun to push the sugar industry; and, not having laid by any of the enormous revenues from cotton, he was forced, in order to carry out his railroad scheme, to contract a seven per cent. loan of £3,000,000, which netted him £2,640,000. The cattle murrain, the abolition of the *corvée*, and his extravagances called for another loan only two years later. The nominal amount of this loan was £11,890,000; but heavier terms had to be made; for, though a seven per cent. stock, it was issued at seventy-five, and yielded, after the usual deductions, only £7,193,334. In other words, the total annual cost of this loan was more than thirteen per cent. "The khédive, by this time," as Mr. McCoan remarks,[1] "was fairly on the road to ruin." But the national credit was

---

[1] McCoan, Egypt As It Is, p. 142.

still good, since the floating debt had been covered by this last loan.

Ismail seems not to have suspected the perils ahead. It was his aim to make a civilized country even out of uncivilized materials, and to develop trade even where natural resources were wanting, let the cost be what it might. It certainly was great; it was enormous. The outlay, even if the revenue of the country had permitted it, would have been foolish extravagance; but in view of Egypt's financial condition, it was nothing less than reckless robbery. The fellahin—the people of Egypt—were the sufferers. The kûrbash exacted more extortionate payments than ever; but all to no purpose. By 1873 the floating liabilities, paying nearly fourteen per cent. interest, amounted to about £26,000,000. The Messrs. Oppenheim, who had secured the loan of 1868, now proposed to fund the entire mass of debts in a seven per cent. loan of £32,000,000. This offer, disastrous in its results, was accepted. The Egyptian government received in cash only £11,740,077, the remainder of the amount realized, £9,000,000, being paid in bonds of the floating debt, which the contractors bought up at a heavy discount and gave over to the Egyptian government at 93. There was, to say the least, a good deal of Shylockism shown by the money-lenders of the West in their financial relations with Egypt. But if they were knavish, Ismail was not altogether simple. Looking at the figures that tell the story of "this wicked waste of a country's resources," as Mr. McCoan calls it, we see that from loans amounting to £58,887,000, the Egyptian government received only £35,437,474. At the end of 1875 the treasury had repaid £29,570,995 in interest and in sinking fund. Was so much money ever paid for so little gain?

There were other loans than those above mentioned. The daira, the immense personal estate of the khédive, afforded excellent security for supplementary loans. The first of these was negotiated in 1866, its amount being £3,387,000. The following year the khédive compelled his uncle Halim to sell to him his inherited estate; and to pay for the property obtained by his enforced sale, the so-called "Mustapha Pasha loan" of £2,080,000 was negotiated. Still another daira loan of more than seven millions sterling was raised in 1870 at seven per cent., the stock being issued at 75. Only £5,000,000 was handed over to the borrower. Thus the same story is told with the private as with the public loans.

The question now was: How long could the ruinous rate of interest be paid on these enormous debts? Up to 1875 it was regularly paid, and the credit of Egypt was good. But the crisis was now near at hand. The stock of the great loan of 1873 was quoted at 53 in the London market, and the Cairene treasury was almost empty. Even Ismail Sadyk, the mûffetish, with all his tortures and threats, could not get piasters enough from the fellahîn to meet the demands that were measured by hundreds of thousands of pounds. And yet he was ordered to find money to pay the December dividend. At this juncture the khédive appealed to England to rescue Egypt from ruin; and produced, as his last card, the 176,000 Suez canal shares, held by his government. The mûffetish was offering the same securities in negotiations with the bankers of Paris and Alexandria, and with the *Crédit Foncier* of France, in his attempt to force upon them new treasury bonds for £16,000,000 at fifteen per cent. interest. After a series of advances and retreats on the part of the English and the French governments, Disraeli's government finally telegraphed to the khédive, in December, 1875, that England would give four millions sterling for the shares in drafts on Rothschild. The offer was eagerly accepted, and the crisis was tided over. The shares of the '73 loan in London rose twenty points at a jump, but after a few days they were quoted at 61, midway between the points of utmost depression and inflation. A more vital interest in the affairs of Egypt was now given to England than she had before possessed. She had gone thither, in the first place, to further the demands of her commerce; she had then manœuvred for the protection of the interests of the British bondholders; and now, in addition to these undertakings, she was to guard the rights that this purchase gave her, and increase the obligations that it heaped upon Egypt.

Four million pounds, as Ismail soon found, could not stem the tide of disaster for long. Everything worth it had been mortgaged, and the mûffetish was offering treasury bonds to the extent of two hundred thousand and three hundred thousand and even four hundred thousand pounds in return for cash advances of one hundred thousand at twenty per cent. A few were taken, and by heavy sales of daira sugar and corn the demands were satisfied for a time. The khédive now invited England to investigate the financial condition of his country, and Mr. Stephen Cave, M.P., was sent out for this purpose. Nubar Pasha, the foremost of Egyptian statesmen, was called to the cabinet, and at the beginning of 1876 everything had a reassuring aspect. But within three months Nubar had resigned, and Disraeli, to the consternation of bondholders, had announced in Parliament that the khédive requested that Mr. Cave's report be not published for fear of its effect upon Egyptian finances. But this request was disregarded. The effect of the report, however, was more favorable to the khédive than he expected, owing to the somewhat rose-colored view Mr. Cave took of the financial outlook.

Egypt [he wrote] may be said to be in a transition state, and she suffers from the defects of the system out of which she is passing as well as from those of the system into which she is attempting to enter. She suffers from the ignorance, dishonesty, waste, and extravagance of the East, such as have brought her suzerain to the verge of ruin, and at the same time from the vast expense caused by hasty and inconsiderate endeavor to adopt the civilization of the West.

He read the causes of Egyptian difficulty aright. But he was wrong in estimating that the yearly revenue from 1876 to 1885 would be more than double the cost of the administration. To meet the necessities of the government, he proposed another unification of all debts, exclusive of three of the earliest and smallest loans which were to be paid off by the operation of the mûkabala. The consolidated debt, amounting to £75,000,000, was to bear interest at seven per cent., and to be redeemable in 1926. The project, however, was not carried out.

The Khédive Ismail, in the meantime, had succeeded in getting the greater part of his floating debt taken up in France. That the holders had been duped was evident before the end of March (1876), for there was no money in the Egyptian treasury to meet the April dividends, and the khédive was appealing for aid to the English and French governments. His overtures were flatly refused by England; but when France realized that the *Crédit Foncier*, the second financial institution of the land, was in a strait in consequence of its relations with Egypt, a cabinet council was summoned in Paris, and on March 31 the April dividend was dispatched to London. And again the impending disaster was averted.

Mr. Cave's scheme for the unification of the debt fell through, as above noticed, although coupled with certain measures of reform, which provided for a regular control of the revenue under the administration of Europeans and natives, and for the establishment of debt and audit officers. The cause of failure was that nominations were left in the hands of the khédive, who was himself controlled by the corrupt mûffetish, Ismail Sadyk. France now proposed a financial scheme; but this also failed of adoption. In November, 1876, however, the English and French bondholders united in sending to Egypt a joint commission, consisting of Mr. Goschen, M.P., and M. Joubert, to solve the financial problem. Their labor resulted in the khédive's issuing a decree, November 18, 1876, that remodelled the debt on the following basis : [1]

TITLE.	AMOUNT.	INTEREST, ETC.	SECURITY.
Unified,	£59,000,000	£4,130,000	General revenues.
Preference,	17,000,000	886,000	Railways, etc.
Daira,	8,825,000	450,000	Khédive's estates.
	£84,825,000	£5,466,000	

The reforms of November 18 secured a substantial power to European comptrollers, and the downfall of Ismail Sadyk, who now disappeared from the face of the earth in the mysterious way common to the Orient. He left an immense property, which included three hundred women in his harem, two hundred and fifty men-servants, £600,000 in money, and 30,000 feddans [2] of land. The mûkabala, which would have been abolished if the unification proposed in May had been accepted, was retained by the Messrs. Goschen and Joubert in a slightly modified form.

Those who fancied that plain sailing was now in store for the khédive and the bondholders were again doomed to disappointment. Within a few months it was apparent that the financial state of affairs was as bad as ever. The ordinary expenses were augmented by a special tax of two shillings

[1] M. G. Mulhall, Egyptian Finance, *The Contemporary Review*, October, 1882.
[2] A feddan is about equal to an acre.

an acre to assist Turkey in the war against Russia. Egypt, backed by England and France, whose interest it was to have all revenues applied to the public debt, for a time resisted the pecuniary demands of the Porte, though she told the Turkish envoys that she would forward troops to the seat of war if the Porte would bear the expenses of transport and maintenance. The new Egyptian parliament, however, at last voted the special war tax, and ten thousand troops were sent at the expense of Egypt.

During 1877 the interest on the loans was raised by collecting the taxes with all the old-time cruelty (Mr. Mulhall says "the fellahin were bastinadoed even more than before"; but that was not possible) and as much as nine months in advance. This ruinous system, of course, brought greater difficulties with each pay-day; and at the beginning of 1878 the outlook, to say the least, was most doleful. It was at this time that the exiled Prince Halim, the uncle of Ismail and the most enlightened, perhaps, of the descent of Mehemet Ali, wrote a letter of advice to Ismail from Constantinople. The letter, which bears the date of March 4, 1878, is worth quoting, at least in part. He wrote:

1. Place the financial administration of the country in the hands of Europeans chosen by the interested powers;

such administration alone having the power to appoint and dismiss all officials connected with the finance of the country.

2. The financial administration thus constituted, and all its dealings being carried on in broad daylight, you must appoint a special inquiry commission, chosen by the high officials, to establish an equitable repartition of taxes, which are now arbitrarily distributed and levied.

3. All property belonging to the princes and princesses shall be made over to the state, so as to be used in payment of all debts.

4. The revenue of all the dairas, the khédive's and his family's, being thus devoted to the paying off of public and private debts, the civil list, the amount of which shall be agreed upon by the interested powers, will support the khédive and his family.

5. The reform tribunals, having over them a sovereign free from all personal interests, and by whose care all the judgments which they pronounce shall be carried out, will be empowered, over and above their present jurisdiction, to try causes between natives, if the latter shall so choose it.

These five articles, says Mr. Jerrold,[1] "became the basis on which the discussion of Egyptian affairs turned." The first article of reform had already met with Ismail's apparent approval, the state revenues having been placed in the hands of two "comptrollers-general," one English and the other French. They were appointed for five years,

[1] Egypt Under Ismail Pasha, p. 256.

with almost unlimited powers in the domain of finance. But the step was taken reluctantly; for the khédive realized that, to quote the words of Mr. Justin McCarthy,[1] "when a country has once accepted an investigation of its finances by foreign powers, and given the practical control of its treasury into the hands of foreign representatives, its claim to independence can hardly fail to be regarded as signally diminished." Still more reluctantly, we may well believe, did the khédive yield to the demand of the commission to hand over his vast private estates to meet the daira coupons. But he had been forced into both of these actions by the troubles of 1877. Early in 1878 the khédive made a bold effort to secure foreign favor and quiet the discontent among the money-lenders of Alexandria. The Egyptian government had announced, in 1877, that it could not pay the existing high rate of interest on the public debt; but before the bondholders would consent to any reduction, they demanded the appointment of a commission to examine into the receipts and expenses of the government. The khédive, in January, 1878, allowed an investigation of receipts, but would permit no examination of expenditures. Two months later, however, he issued the following decree:

[1] England Under Gladstone, ch. xiii.

We, Khédive of Egypt—with respect to our decree of the 27th of January, 1878, instituting a superior Commission of Inquiry, considering that it is the duty of that Commission to prepare and submit for our sanction regulations to secure the regular working of the public services, and to give a just satisfaction to the interests of the country, and to the public creditors—have decreed and do decree :

ARTICLE 1. The widest powers are given to the Commission we establish.

ART. 2. The investigation of the Commission of Inquiry will embrace all the elements of the financial situation, always respecting the legitimate rights of the Government.

ART. 3. The ministers and officials of our Government will be bound to furnish directly to the Commission, at its request and without delay, all information required from them.

ART. 4. There are named as members of the superior Commission of Inquiry: President, M. Ferdinand de Lesseps ; Vice-President, Mr. Rivers Wilson ; Vice-President, his Excellency, Riaz Pasha ; M. Baravelli ; Mr. Baring ; M. de Blignières ; M. de Kremer.

ART. 5. A credit necessary for the expenses of the Commission will be opened on the budget of 1878, in accordance with the report which the President will present us.

ISMAIL.

CAIRO, March 30, 1878.

On August 20, Mr. Rivers Wilson presented the report of the commission of inquiry. The report considered first the system of accounts employed by the Egyptian government. It then explained the system of taxation, and discussed the *corvée*, the military conscription, and the water laws. The second part of the report was taken up with the estimate of the non-consolidated liabilities. The amount of floating debt to be settled was found to be £6,276,000. The gross expenditure for 1878 was estimated at £10,405,665, and the gross receipts at £7,819,000. Adding the difference between receipts and expenditures, £2,586,665, to the amount of floating debt, the total deficit for 1878 would appear to be £8,862,665; but this sum was reduced to a little more than six millions sterling by deductions for security against partially guaranteed debts, and for amounts nominally due to the dairas, but before that time surrendered. There was immediate need, therefore, for about six millions. The report closed with the following suggestions of reform:

That no taxes shall be imposed or gathered without a law, authorizing them, being promulgated; that future legislation may extend the taxation to foreigners; that there shall be an efficient control over tax-collectors; that there shall be a reserve fund to provide against the contingency of a bad rising of the Nile; that there shall be a special jurisdiction for complaints on the subject of the collection and assessment of taxes for the special protection of the natives; that existing vexatious taxes shall be abolished, except for works of public utility; that the obligation to military service shall be placed under restrictions; and that all the immovable property of the different dairas, shall be independently managed by a special administration for the benefit of the creditors both of the state and the dairas.

These were excellent recommendations, though there was something very naïve in the suggestion that "there shall be a *reserve fund* to provide against the contingency of a bad rising of the Nile." It would have been as easy to resolve that, if the river failed to rise, copious rains should fall; for reserve funds are as rare in Egypt as rain-storms in the desert. Not the least good of the recommendations was that providing that foreigners should be taxed; a measure that the Westerners have always been shamefully slow to encourage. The reforms contained also a plan for the cadastral survey of Egypt, which was recognized in England, in France, and in Egypt, as just to the fellahin and as the treasury's only safeguard against fraud and corruption. The khédive accepted the report on August 23 in a speech expressing entire approval of the work of the commission, appreciation of their services, and determination to carry out the reforms. To show how thoroughly in earnest he was, so he said, he had recalled Nubar Pasha from exile and would entrust him with the formation of a new ministry. The new ministry was composed of the following persons : Nubar Pasha, president of the council, minister of foreign affairs and of justice; Riaz Pasha, minister of interior ; Ratif Pasha, minister of war; Ali Mubarek Pasha, minister of public instruction, agriculture, and public works. The portfolio of finance was left vacant, but it was soon offered to Mr. Rivers Wilson, who accepted the office with the consent of the British government. This excited the jealousy of France, to appease which the comparatively unimportant office of public works was offered to M. de Blignières. Italy then put in the claim that she should be consulted in Egyptian affairs ; but her voice was ignored.

Before any active steps had been taken toward inaugurating the proposed reforms, Mr. Wilson urged the necessity of another loan to meet immediate demands, and this, although the total debt already amounted to ninety-two millions sterling. But he had no choice in the matter ; the loan was imperative. The only unmortgaged property on which a loan could be raised consisted of the daira estates belonging to the khédive's family. These, now, with a rent-roll of £430,000 a year, were handed over to the state, in consequence, not of the advice of Prince Halim, but of the utter necessity of the time. The loan was concluded with the Messrs. Rothschild of Paris, in November, 1878, at the rate of 73. The nominal amount of the loan was

£8,500,000, but with the discount of twenty-seven per cent. and the commission of two and a half per cent., the net product was only £5,992,000. Thinking that financial affairs could rest for the moment, Mr. Wilson now made a tour of inspection through Lower Egypt. The people met him with petitions, which he received with promises of redress. He believed, and they had every reason to believe, the words he uttered in a speech at Tanta.

A new era [he said] has begun for Egypt. Reforms are already initiated, and if you will only have patience, you can count on their completion. If you have grievances, make them known to us, and you shall be righted. We wish to establish equality and legality in the country, and the law shall no longer be for the rich alone; it shall work for rich and poor alike.

The fellahín might well have been happy; they had never in their ages of oppression received such assurances before.

But tranquillity was not yet. A number of creditors at Alexandria had put an end to the financial negotiations in a most unexpected manner. These creditors had been watching their opportunity. They had tried some months before to seize the furniture of the palace at Ramleh, but had been foiled by the bailiffs. They had succeeded, however, in obtaining a lien on the very estates that were offered as security for the new loan. It was not surprising, therefore, that Baron Rothschild withheld the amount of the loan. To add to the khédive's troubles, the unpaid officers of the army in Cairo were urging their claims. The delay of Baron Rothschild precipitated matters; and on February 18, 1879, a military uprising occurred in Cairo, which nearly cost Mr. Rivers Wilson and Nubar Pasha their lives. While driving from a council of ministers their carriage was beset by a throng of officers, estimated at from four to twelve hundred; their driver was wounded, and they were insulted and forced back into the court-yard of the palace. The khédive attempted to pacify the mob, but they were only dispersed by the force of arms. Nubar Pasha, the next day, offered his resignation. It was at once accepted by the khédive, and again the foremost statesman of Egypt, and the only one worthy the name, according to the Western conception of the term, went into exile. It was immediately claimed in England and France that Ismail had sought to bring about this result by instigating or conniving at the insurrection among the officers. It was generally known that Ismail had a pet aversion to Nubar. They were as different as an honest man and a cunning diplomat could well be, and it is certain that the khédive would not have entrusted Nubar with the new ministry if the influence of England and France had not seemed to demand it. Confidence having been secured, Ismail was ready, and probably only too glad, to break with his prime-minister. Nubar appreciated the desperate state of affairs that prevailed in Egypt. He had written to a friend on January 20 :

The everlasting political comedy, or tragedy, is being played on the little stage here, just as it is everywhere else : a lost power sought to be regained, persons interested in not letting it be regained, who yet aid it for personal motives, or to give themselves importance—and not a sou in the Treasury withal. What a situation for the country, for the interested countries, and for your friend!'

England and France were naturally displeased with the dismissal—for such it was—of Nubar Pasha ; and while the commander-in-chief of the Egyptian army was apologizing to Mr. Rivers Wilson for the insult he had received at the hands of the officers, the two powers were preparing a protest to submit to the khédive. Notwithstanding their demand, Nubar was not reinstated ; but some of the conditions they imposed upon the khédive were followed in his attitude toward the new cabinet. Ismail's eldest son, Prince Tewfik, was appointed president of the council, Zulfikar Pasha minister of foreign affairs, and Mr. Wilson and M. de Blignières were retained in their former offices. The

¹ Quoted from Appleton's *Annual Cyclopædia*, 1879.

important condition that was imposed upon Ismail was embraced by him in a letter to Tewfik, in which he said : " As the native ministers now form a majority in the cabinet, it is right, in order to restore the balance of power and lend to the intervention of our European ministers all the usefulness possible, that they should be entitled to a veto on all measures they agree in disapproving." This sop thrown to the great powers was soon counteracted. Egyptian and European influence clashed on the financial question, and Egypt came out first best. It was in this wise : Mr. Wilson, M. de Blignières, Mr. Baring, and the debt commissioners submitted a plan for the equitable reduction of the claims of all creditors. The khédive opposed this with another plan, giving the bondholders better terms ; and he was supported by the native parliament, the pashas, the ulemas, and all the high dignitaries of the land. The counter projects were pushed so hard that, on April 7, Prince Tewfik resigned the presidency of the council, and the khédive dismissed Mr. Wilson and M. de Blignières.

If, now, there was ever a ship of state that sailed between Scylla and Charybdis, it was the unsteady craft that Ismail was trying to guide. If he avoided the rocks on one side, it was only to meet destruction on the other. The wrath of the Egyptians had been averted by the dismissal of the foreigners, and by the same act the wrath of the great powers had been incurred. The French government was in high dudgeon at the offence, and threatened to reinstate her representative by force of arms, and asked England to join her. But England would not agree to any such decisive step. Even had she cared to, she would have found it difficult to spare more troops than were needed at that time to oppose the Boers in South Africa. She preferred, therefore, while waiting for the blood of France to cool, to send dispatches to the khédive, demanding a reconsideration of his hasty and unwarranted action. But the khédive was now running things with a high hand. If England would not allow France to send an armed force to Egypt, and did not do so herself, he could laugh at the demands and threats of dispatches. His people said that the unbelievers had brought all the trouble and the ruin upon the fair valley of the Nile, and he decided to cut loose from the Western influence and defy its power. He virtually repudiated the debts and responsibilities of his country in a way that would put our own Virginia to shame, by issuing a decree, April 22, in which he declared that, for the future, he would himself control the finances and regulate the discharge of liabilities. He seemed to be riding on the wave of triumph. The people thought that the day of Mehemet Ali was come again.

But at this moment an unexpected voice of authority was heard. England and France were passing the time in an unavailing effort like that of two horses who cannot pull their load because the one holds back while the other starts, when, suddenly, the German chancellor made a protest that cost Ismail his throne. The German consul at Cairo, on the 17th of May, simply informed the khédive that the interests of German subjects must be protected, let come what might, and that any arbitrary change of system at that time would be considered prejudicial to their interests. What led the astute Bismarck to take the lead at this juncture is, and will probably remain, an enigma.[1]

[1] Of this action and its consequences, Mr. Edward Dicey, writing in *The Nineteenth Century* of February, 1880, says: " How this action came about has never, so far as I know, been clearly ascertained. Germany had a comparatively insignificant interest in the affairs of Egypt. A very small portion of the floating debt was due to German creditors. It is not easy to believe that Germany ever really contemplated any intervention in Egypt, and it is still less easy to understand how she could practically have intervened even if she had been so minded. But the prestige of Germany—her repute of strength, which is to a nation what credit is to an individual— stood her in good stead. The mere fact that Prince Bismarck had declared the khédive could not be allowed to play fast and loose with the interests of German subjects produced more effect than all the dispatches indited from London and Paris ; and from the day when Germany pronounced against the khédive it was obvious that the end had come. Meanwhile, the initiative taken by Germany had a result which might easily have been foreseen, and which doubtless was foreseen by those, whoever they may have been, who suggested to Prince Bismarck the advisability of his coming forward as the champion of the Egyptian creditors. It was felt at once in Paris that the time for vacillation had passed. The Republic could not allow it to be said

Doubtless he wished France still to be occupied with foreign affairs, so that her internal development might not be commensurate with Germany's; for at that day, more than now, there seemed a plausible possibility that the grievances and hatred that did not die with Napoleon Third might seek again a settlement by the sword. Certain it is that the very reasons that have led England to oppose French aggrandizement abroad, have led Germany to favor the same, or, at least, to view with satisfaction the foreign complications that require the exportation of troops and treasure. Against France, England has had to protect only her interests abroad, and Germany her interests at home. This may or may not account for the chancellor's unexpected though timely interference; but the fact remains the same that his voice settled the khédive's fate. England, France, Austria, Russia, and Italy followed the lead of Germany, and protested against any interference with the commission of control and the non-execution of the tribunal judgments. At this juncture the proposal to depose

that France was unable or unwilling to protect the interests of her subjects in Egypt, while the insignificant interests of the German creditors were safeguarded by the mere expression of Prince Bismarck's will; and the English government recognized, on the one hand, that France could not be held back any longer, and, on the other, that we could not allow Germany to take into her own hands the forcible solution of the Egyptian question."

the khédive, which the Porte had made to England and France in April, was renewed. This time it was accepted. In place, however, of the sultan's nominee for the succession—Prince Halim, the uncle of Ismail—England and France insisted upon raising Prince Tewfik, the son of Ismail, to the throne. The diplomatic correspondence in discussion of this difference consumed a week or more in June; but on the 26th of that month the sultan at last yielded and signed the firman deposing Ismail in favor of Prince Mehemet Tewfik. Four days afterward the ex-khédive left the shores and troubles of Egypt behind him for an Italian life of luxury. If he had been a pasha in the feudal days of Egypt, he would have forfeited his treasure and his life. As it was, he escaped with the latter, and was given an annual allowance of £50,000.

The character of Ismail Pasha has been variously depicted. He has been painted with all the virtues, on the one hand, and all the vices, on the other, that a monarch can be heir to. Of course neither extreme gives the true picture; and yet there is so much ground for each conception, that one inclines, at first thought, to declare that Ismail was both the blessing and the curse of his country. We think of the development of Egypt during the sixteen years of his reign, of the public works, schools, railways, telegraphs, founded and fostered, and we bless his name ; but then we think of the cost, and the curse follows. We cannot agree with those who would shield Ismail by regarding him as the dupe of his wicked mûffetish. He may have been deceived and cheated by the latter, but he could not have been altogether ignorant of the financial schemes of his treasurer. They worked in the same groove and to the same end. They were both ambitious, but were not equally extravagant ; for the mûffetish grew rich correspondingly as the khédive grew poor, although the money poured into the hands of the two alike. The mûffetish hoarded while the khédive wasted ; but the desire of the miser was no greater than that of the spendthrift, and he must not bear the blame for both. For the financial woes of Egypt under Ismail some blame, undoubtedly, attaches to the European money-lenders, whose bargains were so disastrous to the khédive. Their rates were often merciless. To prove that all the blame is theirs, Mr. Keay tells *A Tale of Shame*,[1] from the British blue books, in which he supports his arguments with many italics, small capitals, and exclamation points. But they are not conclusive. They do not obliterate the fact of Ismail's extravagance.

If we could wholly lose sight of the different acts

[1] J. Seymour Keay, Spoiling the Egyptians : A Tale of Shame. Told from the Blue Books.

of the financial tragedy, the glory of Ismail's reign would still be marred by the means and measures he employed in carrying out his designs of development. No obstacle could turn him from his plan, and the teachings of economic science were ignored or misunderstood. We have seen how he bent his energies upon the senseless attempt to refine sugar, when his country furnished no fuel to run his dearly bought machines. Western civilization was Ismail's model in all things. It was his ambition, from the start, to implant in Egypt European arts and ideas. He thought he could declare into existence what had been the slow development of centuries in more enlightened lands. Even when he must have known that his country was on the verge of ruin, he boasted that Egypt was no longer a part of Africa, but of Europe.[1] Nothing could be more ridiculous than the story of Ismail's attempt to give his people governmental representation. He did not propose to establish even a paper constitution; and he had no idea of giving up any of his prerogatives, when, in 1866, he summoned the first Egyptian parliament that had assembled since the day of Mehemet Ali.[2]

[1] In an interview with Mr. Rivers Wilson, August 23, 1877, Ismail said: "My country is no longer African; we now form part of Europe." From *Annual Cyclopædia* for 1877.

[2] Mr. McCoan, in Egypt As It Is, page 117, thus describes the functions of the assembly: "In 1866, the Khédive revived the defunct Assembly of Delegates, one of the inchoate reforms projected by Mehemet Ali, but

The members of the new parliament had not the faintest idea of their duties and powers. When the first bill was submitted to them by the khédive, and they were asked to signify their approval or disapproval, there was not a dissenting vote against the measure. For, they said, his Highness is the representative of Allah; and his will, like that of Allah and the Prophet, is our law. But this political simplicity vanished before the end of Ismail's reign, though the voice of the parliament was still recognized as the khédive's voice.

It is only fair to Ismail that a somewhat detailed statement should be made of the amounts expended by him in public works; for, having seen how one loan after another was received, the question naturally arises: Where did the money go? There was a considerable sum that the greed of money-lenders did not absorb in commissions and interest, and a large part of this went into public works. Mr. Mulhall gives the following table of works established between 1863 and 1879, in his article on " Egyptian Finance ":[1]

which had not met since his death. This germ of an Egyptian Parliament consists of village sheikhs and other provincial notables, elected by the communes, and assembles once a year to receive from the Privy Council a report on the administration during the twelvemonth. Its function is also to consider and advise on all proposed fiscal changes, new public works, and other matters of national concern that may be laid before it. It has, of course, no legislative power; but in practice its recommendations are received not merely with respect, but are often acted on by the Government."

[1] *Contemporary Review*, October, 1882.

Work.	Amount.	Observation.
Suez canal . . .	£6,770,000	After deducting value of shares sold.
Nile canals . . .	12,600,000	Made 8,400 miles at £1,500 per mile.
Bridges	2,150,000	Built 430 at £5,000 per bridge.
Sugar-mills . . .	6,100,000	Built 64, with machinery, *etc.*
Harbor Alexandria	2,542,000	Greenfield and Elliot, contract.
Suez docks . . .	1,400,000	Dussaud Bros.
Alex. water-works	300,000	Price agreed by Paris Syndicate.
Railways . . .	13,361,000	Length 910 miles, new.
Telegraphs . . .	853,000	Length 5,200 miles, new.
Lighthouses . . .	188,000	Built 15 on Red Sea and Mediterranean.
	£46,264,000	

We see thus that Ismail expended on works of public utility not less than forty-six millions sterling. Now, as the loans contracted by him netted only about forty-five millions, his admirers and defenders say at once that he did not squander, but that he spent all for the public weal. But there is the item of revenue, which these writers do not consider, and which yielded the government, in the sixteen years of Ismail's reign, not far from one hundred and fifty millions. How large a part of this was wasted by Ismail we can only guess ; but we may be sure that all those millions did not go toward defraying necessary governmental expenses. The canals, railways, bridges, docks, *etc.*, were the best work of Ismail's reign if the financial side of the question be left out of consideration. They brought in, it is true, a certain revenue, but this was by no means equal to the interest on the debts incurred to make the improvements. Where national development is only secured by contracting with each change a counterbalancing debt, it is doubtful if the changes can be considered beneficial. There were, however, certain other outlays by Ismail that were of unquestionable advantage to the land, even though they produced no revenue. He established 4,632 public schools, with 5,850 teachers, drawing salaries that ranged from £24 to £84 a year, and expended in the sixteen years of his reign no less than £3,600,000 for this purpose. He organized village banks—we will say with philanthropic intent to protect the fellahin from the money-lenders—and lost £900,000 by the experiment. And he lost largely on the shares he took in the Nile Steam Navigation Company. On the other hand, just at the time of the financial difficulties of 1873, he embarked upon a war with Abyssinia which despoiled the Egyptian treasury of not less than £3,000,000. He squandered a vast sum in building palaces and theatres and in the entertainment of distinguished foreigners. His expenditures at the time of the opening of the Suez canal were simply enormous. He gave bribes and presents at all times with true Oriental prodigality. Even if he could have afforded these outlays, they would have been foolish; as it was, they were wicked. And yet, as Mr. Mulhall says, "whatever the faults, he raised Egypt in the scale of nations"; for there was an actual progress between the death of Said and the accession of Tewfik. It may be measured in the following table, prepared by Mr. Mulhall:[1]

PROGRESS OF EGYPT IN SEVENTEEN YEARS.

	LAST YEAR OF SAID PASHA. 1862.	LAST YEAR OF ISMAIL PASHA. 1879.
Acres tilled	4,052,000	5,425,000
Value of imports	£1,991,000	£5,410,000
Value of exports	£4,454,000	£13,810,000
Revenue	£4,937,000	£8,562,000
Public debt	£3,300,000	£98,540,000
Number of public schools	185	4,817
Railways—miles	275	1,185
Telegraphs "	630	5,820
Canals "	44,000	52,400
Population "	4,883,000	5,518,000

If from this table could be excluded that decidedly negative item of progress denoted by the public debt in 1879, there would remain a good showing for Ismail; but that one item cancels all the others, even as it was the primal cause of Ismail's overthrow.

There was another reform, which has not yet been noticed because bearing no direct relation to finances, that was accomplished during Ismail's reign, and for which he must, at least indirectly, be credited — the reform in judicial procedure. There had come to be a very pernicious increase

[1] *Contemporary Review*, October, 1882.

of consular jurisdiction in Egypt after the death of Mehemet Ali. The native had to bring a suit against a foreigner in the foreigner's consulate, where he was almost sure to be denied justice. With as little chance of justice, also, the foreign plaintiff had to sue the foreign debtor in the latter's consulate. Some consuls even claimed the right to sit in judgment of cases in which the natives were defendants. The government suffered too. It was estimated, says Mr. McCoan,[1] that, in the four years preceding 1868, consular influence extorted from the government £2,880,000 in satisfaction of claims, without judicial sanction of any kind. "The whole system," he goes on to say, "was, in fact, a scandal and a denial of justice all around." It was, if anything, worse in criminal than in civil matters. The abuses were so flagrant that Nubar Pasha, in 1867, proposed a scheme of reform to the khédive. It was submitted to France, but was unfavorably received. England, however, when approached on the subject, promised to give the reform her hearty support, provided the other powers would concur. They did so in the fall of 1869. Negotiations, however, were interrupted for a time by the war between France and Germany; and when they were renewed, in 1871, the sultan entered his veto against

[1] Egypt As It Is, p. 276.

the scheme, though he afterward withdrew it at the demand of England and Russia. France now offered objections once more, and the negotiations dragged. Some of her amendments were accepted; but it was not until December, 1875, that the scheme was finally agreed to.

The reform was inaugurated in February, 1876, to continue in force for five years. It is thus described by Mr. McCoan:[1]

As now constituted the new system includes three tribunals of first instance—one at Alexandria, a second at Cairo, and a third . . . at Zagazig—and a Court of Appeal, which also sits at Alexandria. Of the inferior courts, that at Alexandria—divided into two chambers, with equal jurisdiction—consists of fourteen judges, of whom six are natives and eight Europeans; that at Cairo, of three natives and five foreigners; and that at Zagazig, of three natives and four foreigners. The nominal chiefs of all three are natives, but foreign vice-presidents actually direct their proceedings. In the Court of Appeal the alien element is still more preponderant, the bench of eleven judges there consisting of seven foreigners and only four natives. . . . The judicial and other personnel is thus complete, and the jurisdiction exercised includes all civil disputes between the government and natives on the one hand and foreigners on the other, as also those between foreigners of different nationalities; and all suits and registrations of sale and mortgage whatsoever of real property.

[1] Egypt As It Is, p. 280.

Such was the reform inaugurated; and a most excellent one it was. Not forgetting that Nubar was its author, we give the credit of it to Ismail's reign, just as we lay the blame of the mûffetish's villany at his door. If all his changes had been as wisely carried out, his ambitious designs of raising Egypt to the plane of European civilization would not have failed so utterly of realization. In this connection we must refer to Ismail's appointment, first of Sir Samuel Baker and then of Colonel Gordon, as governors-general of the Sûdan and of his apparently earnest attempts to suppress the slave trade. He gave Gordon unlimited power to " punish, change, and dismiss" officials, and assured him that Egypt would loyally support England in this " measure of humanity and civilization." We shall see later how Baker and Gordon succeeded in their missions.

Long before his collapse the shrewd Ismail must have known that his reign was doomed; but he kept on his high-handed course to the end. The discharge of the European administrators and the virtual repudiation of debts were his last acts of bravado. Powerless and empty-handed, he made no protest against the firman of deposition. But "it would be a mistake," writes Mr. Edward Dicey "to attribute Ismail Pasha's collapse to lack of personal courage.

[1] *The Nineteenth Century*, February, 1880.

I should doubt his possessing any exceptional physical bravery; but he had to a remarkable degree the gambler's instinct and the gambler's boldness. He was not the man to forfeit his stakes while there was a chance, however remote, of holding on to his winnings. He threw up the game simply and solely because he knew better than any one else that he had absolutely no cards in his hand." His people suffered him to depart into exile without a protest or a murmur. It is true that "the resident European community"—to quote Mr. Dicey's words once more—" to whom he had always been friendly, and who had partaken freely of his lavish hospitality, stood by him in his disgrace, and his departure into exile was accompanied by sincere expressions of regret on the part of the court circle and the European embassy, but without one solitary manifestation of sympathy on the part of the Egyptian population."

IV.

MEHEMET TEWFIK, KHÉDIVE.

PRINCE MEHEMET TEWFIK was not yet twenty-seven years old when he ascended the vice-royal throne of Egypt. He was a very different man from his father. He had not his inordinate ambition, and lacked, consequently, some of the energy as well as the crafty diplomacy of Ismail. He had not, like his father, served an apprenticeship of experience in the gay capitals of Europe; but he was not without the culture that European masters can inspire. He had a good knowledge of French and English, speaking both languages fluently. It may be doubted if he was as enlightened a prince as his great uncle, Prince Halim, the èxile of Constantinople, who was the choice of the sultan for successor to Ismail; but under the law of succession in Egypt, established by the firman of 1866, England could not well have supported Halim, even if she had preferred him, which she did not. The Porte had to yield. Its eagerness to depose Ismail is not to be attributed to any over-sensitiveness at the scandal of his financial follies, but rather to the fact—which the sultan foresaw—that if the Porte did not depose the khédive, England and France would. Making, thus, a concession to the inevitable, the sultan would have still maintained the semblance of his suzerain authority if he could have named the successor. But this was not permitted by England and France, who, by their dictation at this time, showed that they possessed the virtual control of affairs in Egypt.

And yet, after the deposition, England at least was loth to put her power further to the test. The opposition at home was to be feared and a definite policy was not outlined; and the new khédive was left to follow his own whim largely in the formation of his government. France did not relish this inaction on the part of England, and, for herself, insisted that M. de Blignières should continue to act as representative. Germany and the other Powers having retired from participation in the discussion of Egyptian affairs, England and France at last came to a compromise. They agreed not to insist upon the reinstatement of their representatives in the khédive's cabinet, but, instead, upon the appointment by the khédive of two comptrollers, one of whom should be nominated by France and the other by England. France named M. de Blignières, who was accepted by Tewfik with much dissatisfaction. England did not insist upon the appointment of Mr. Rivers Wilson, though losing thereby some prestige, but named Major Baring instead. Their powers were not defined ; but it was understood that they would be as unlimited as France and England might choose to make them.

In the meantime there had been several ministerial changes since Tewfik's accession. He had placed the ministry under the leadership of Sherif Pasha. None but natives received portfolios. The ministry thus formed indicated a reactionary spirit, and was totally out of sympathy with the reform movement instigated by Nubar Pasha. Tewfik feared to depart at once from the ways of Ismail ; for he regarded his position as somewhat insecure so long as Ismail's covert overtures to the Porte were received. The ex-khédive sought to obtain permission of the sultan to live in Cairo. This could not have been allowed without prejudicing the stability of the Egyptian government ; but all fear of the possibility was ended when, on August 14, the firman of investiture was presented to Tewfik. Four days after, the Sherif ministry was dismissed and a new one formed, of which the khédive himself assumed the presidency. But this was short-lived ; for, on September 21, Tewfik gave up his position of minister and appointed Riaz Pasha to the presidency in his place. Riaz had been minister of the interior under Nubar, with whom he was in complete sympathy. It would seem, however, as if the ministry should have been intrusted to Nubar, the most enlightened man of Egypt ; but Riaz was preferred by France and England because, in case of differences arising, he would hardly have the courage or strength to oppose the Dual Control, which was a consideration of some moment now that the Powers had no representatives in the cabinet. Then, too, Nubar was not popular among the natives, being an Armenian and a Christian. At the same time that the khédive's government was placed upon an apparently stable footing, the burdens of the fellahin were materially lightened by unusually abundant crops. They were also less harassed than formerly by the tax-gatherers, who no longer forced money from them a year or more before it was due, but were content merely to collect arrearages. There seemed thus to be a brighter sky above Egypt than in the days of Ismail Pasha.

But there was the great question of finance still remaining to be solved. To this the comptrollers turned their first attention. The difficulty that met them at the outset was of an international character. It will be remembered that Baron Rothschild had withheld a part of his loan at the beginning of the year, because individual creditors had obtained liens against the daira domains, which Ismail and his family had ceded to the state. The domains could not be mortgaged to the Rothschilds until the liens had been satisfied; for their legality had been upheld by the International Courts, whose law was that of a code based upon French law. This code, now, could not be deviated from or modified in the least degree except with the consent of all the Powers represented in the International Courts. But it was evidently a matter of right and necessity that funds borrowed to lighten certain burdens of the state should be expended to that end and not in the payment of the claims of individuals. An independent Power would have so decided at once; but Egypt had to abide by the code, while the comptrollers proceeded to try to secure the consent of the Powers concerned. This was a difficult task. Some of the lesser Powers were jealous of the Anglo-French control, and had no desire to act upon its bidding. Italy and Austria declined to sanction any change in the international code. Major Baring and M. de Blignières themselves went to Vienna to expostulate, and with the strong influence of the nations they represented they were at last able, in November, to effect a compromise, by which all the liens on the domains, obtained before their mortgage to the Rothschilds on February 3, 1879, were to be satisfied from the unpaid balance of the loan; while, with respect to all other debts, the Rothschilds were to have the first mortgage on the lands. This was accomplished only by tedious negotiations. In the month of November, also, the khédive issued the following decree concerning the powers of the comptrollers-general:

ARTICLE 1. The Comptrollers-General shall have in financial matters the most complete powers of investigation into all the public services, including those whose receipts have a special destination by virtue of decrees and contracts. Ministers and functionaries of every rank shall be bound to give every information and to furnish every document required by the Comptrollers and their agents. The Minister of Finance especially shall furnish the Control every week with a detailed statement of all receipts and expenditures at his Ministry. Every other Administration shall every month furnish a similar statement of receipts and expenditures.

ART. 2. The Comptrollers shall agree upon the public services over which they shall exercise the rights of supervision and control conferred by this decree.

ART. 3. The Governments of France and Great Britain having consented, for the moment, that the Comptrollers shall take no part in the management of the Administration and financial services, the Comptrollers shall for the present confine themselves to the communication to us or to our Ministers of such observations as their investigations give rise to. They shall also communicate to the Commission of the Debt all facts of a nature to interest the creditors of the consolidated Debt. They may also, on account of such facts, convene the Commissioners of Public Debt to examine such questions as the Comptrollers or the Commissioners of Public Debt may think advisable to discuss in common.

ART. 4. The Comptrollers shall have the rank of Ministers at the Council [of Ministers], and shall have a seat and a consultive voice there.

ART. 5. At the end of each year, and more frequently if necessary, the Comptrollers shall communicate to us their work in a report, which shall be published by them and inserted in the *Moniteur Égyptien*.

ART. 6. The Comptrollers can only be removed from their posts with the consent of their respective Governments. They shall name their own officials and fix their salaries.

ART. 7. The expenses of the department of the Control shall be fixed by the Comptrollers and approved by the Ministers.

ART. 8. The amount required by them shall be paid to them monthly.

ART. 9. Our Ministers are charged with the execution of this decree.

[Signed]   MEHEMET TEWFIK,
                   RIAZ PASHA.

November 15, 1879.

The remainder of the year 1879 was consumed by the comptrollers in drafting a plan for the settlement of the financial question. Their report was presented to the khédive in January, 1880. Its most important suggestion was that a line of demarcation should be drawn at December 31, 1879; and that all debts contracted before that date should be settled by a law of liquidation, which should protect the Egyptian government from all suits based on claims of earlier date than 1880. It had been understood, when the comptrollers were appointed the previous summer, that a committee of liquidation should be instituted to draft such a law as the comptrollers now suggested and, further, to devise some such scheme for the final settlement of financial difficulties as was outlined in the report of the comptrollers. The commission was now appointed with the approval of England, France, Italy, Austria, Germany, and Egypt, and Sir Rivers Wilson was chosen its president. The khédive, in a decree issued in March, outlined the duties of the commission. It was to investigate thoroughly the finances of the country, to draw up a law of liquidation between Egypt and her creditors which should be binding on all concerned, and to make general provision to ease Egypt of her burdens. The governments represented in the commission agreed to accept its decisions as binding on the International Courts, and to request jointly, after having given their own approval, that the other Powers represented in the International Courts should also consent to the new law.

The work of the commission was completed by the middle of July, and the khédive at once signed the law of liquidation. It provided for the payment of the floating debt by giving thirty per cent. cash and seventy per cent. in the bonds of a new preference debt. The national debt was converted into unified and preference stock, the former bearing interest at four per cent. and the latter at five per cent. The unified stock, amounting to £57,776,340, was secured by the land tax, and the preference stock, amounting to £22,587,800, was secured by the railways, telegraphs, *etc.* The daira debt of £9,512,870, and the domain debt of £8,499,620 were secured respectively by the khédive's estates and his family's estates. The mûkabala amounted to £7,500,000. The entire indebtedness was thus placed at over one hundred and five millions sterling. The mûkabala tax was abolished, and a source of revenue cut off; but it was thought that the daira, being freed now from debt, could be made to yield a revenue enough larger to counterbalance the loss of the mûkabala tax. The khédive had previously signed decrees abolishing this tax and certain others that had been declared by the commissioners of inquiry to be annoying to the tax-payer and of little profit to the state. The relief to Egypt by the new law was to be found in the reduction of the interest on the unified debt to four per cent. That would at once bring the expenses of the government below the sum of the revenues and furnish a surplus that could be applied to the service of the debt. The practical working of the law secured this very result. In 1881, after the discharge of all obligations, there remained a surplus of £321,265, which enabled the government to cancel nearly half a million of the funded debt. "The Liquidation Law of 1880," says Mr. Mulhall,[1] "first put the finances on a sound footing and . . . its effects have been just and beneficial."

Other causes, also, worked to secure the prosperity of 1880. There was an abundant harvest, and trade was vastly improved by the readjustment of the land tax and by the abolition of taxes in kind. In short, the condition of the fellah was substantially bettered; and when the fellah is happy, Egypt prospers. The improvement in the national credit was the cause of a great influx of foreign capital, chiefly from France, which was directed toward the development of the agricultural resources of the land and toward the erection of buildings and the improvement of mechanical appliances. Money was loaned at a lower rate of interest than formerly, and as a consequence the price of land rose rapidly. At the same time attention was roused to secure the advancement of the people by giving them better facilities for education. The great Moslem university of Cairo instructed twelve thousand students in the philosophy of the Koran,

[1] *The Contemporary Review*, October, 1882.

but gave them no broader education than the word of the Prophet required. This was not enough for a country that was no longer isolated from the laws and learning of unbelievers, as it had been for the centuries preceding. The actual contact with European nations now made it necessary to cultivate the learning of the West. A commission was appointed to secure this end.

But the reform and prosperity were not to be without their hindrances. The Egyptians had had little thought for themselves while their condition seemed hopeless. Suffering, they were content to exist. But now their prosperity seemed to arouse the prejudices of race and religion and stirred the people to complain of the foreign influence and interference in Egypt. And though the prosperity was, as we have seen, in large part due to the foreign direction, there was some natural ground for complaint. The people could not look without envy and jealousy on the foreigners who were drawing immense salaries from the Egyptian treasury. Fifty thousand pounds a year was paid to European officials in the national debt office alone.[1] There

---

[1] The following salaries paid to foreign officials in the different departments were reported by Sir Edward Malet to his government on May 18, 1882: Cabinet of the Khédive, £3,000 (Egyptian pounds, £1 being about equal to $5); Maieh Sanieh, £676; Presidency of the Council of Ministers, £452; Teft of Gizeh and Gizereh, £436; Ministry of Foreign Affairs, £2,088; Ministry of Finance, £17,200; General Control, £14,101; Di-

might not have been complaint if salaries had gone solely to comptrollers, commissioners, and judges ; but there were, besides, French or English officials to direct the customs, the railways, the telegraphs, the harbors of Alexandria, of Port Said, and of Suez, the coast-guard, the light-houses, the post-office, the finance department of the government, the public works, and the administration of the domain and daira lands. In all these offices, furthermore, the subordinate positions were divided almost equally between Frenchmen and natives. Major Baring had been replaced by Mr. Colvin as English comptroller, and M. de Blignières had assumed the lead in control in consequence of his seniority and greater experience in Egyptian affairs. In every way

rection of the Cadastral Survey, £26,787 ; General Inspection of the Octrois, £2,770; Light-House Service, £10,239 ; Mint, £144 ; Ministry of War, £8,351 ; Ministry of Marine, £2,691 ; Ministry of Public Instruction, £7,905 ; Administration of the Wakfij, £2,034; Ministry of the Interior, £3,978; Government of Alexandria, £780 ; of Port Said, £870 ; of Suez, £163 ; of El Arish, £84 ; Municipality of Alexandria, £540 ; Cairo Police, £1,567 ; Alexandria Police, £2,793 ; Suppression of the Slave Trade, £2,052 ; Marine Sanitary Council and Quarantine, £5,290 ; Council of Public Health, £6,084 ; Ministry of Justice, £6,848 ; Ministry of Public Works, £26,216 ; Railroad Administration, £29,761 ; Telegraph Administration, £6,193 ; Port of Alexandria, £3,681 ; Administration of Customs, £16,647 ; Administration of the Port, £19,509 ; Postal Steamer, £16,941 ; Salines, £162 ; Administration of the Public Domain, £25,042 ; Daira Sanieh, £19,672 ; Public Debt, £16,227 ; Parquet Administration, £3,083 ; Court of Appeals, £14,971 ; Alexandria Court of the First Instance, £22,344 ; Court of the First Instance at Cairo, £14,212 ; Court of the First Instance at Mansûrah, £8,869. Total, £373,491.

France had been more aggressive than her ally, and hers was now the leading influence in Egypt. It was even whispered that the prophecy that the Mediterranean would one day be "a French lake" was destined to fulfillment. French accessions in northern Africa encouraged this kind of talk. But it mattered not to the Egyptians whether French or English controlled : they were all alike foreigners, and on that account hated. Both were bad, and either was as bad as the other. That they were apparently robbing the natives of the salaries that seemed rightfully theirs was enough to make the inborn hatred intense.

The khédive, however, had more tolerance for the foreigners and more sympathy with the reforms they suggested. He believed that the comptrollers had the welfare of Egypt at heart, and he was ready to show his confidence by awaiting the development of the plans undertaken. This attitude, of course, tended to alienate the khédive from his people. Among them a national feeling had been aroused. During 1881 this feeling was crystallized into a recognized national movement, which was to culminate, in 1882, in the cry of "Egypt for the Egyptians." There was only one place where this movement could take form, and that was in the army. Up to 1881 this was still composed almost entirely of Egyptians ; but with the accession of Tewfik, in

1879, the army's grievances had begun. The sultan, notwithstanding the firman that Ismail had so dearly purchased, insisted upon enforcing military restrictions. The limit of enlistment was placed at 18,000 men. Next to the interference of France or England, that of the Porte was most unpopular among Egyptians. The curtailment of the army, however, might have been endured; but the innovations that were begun with 1881 were unbearable. The special grievance was the replacement of native officers by Turks.

The leading spirit among the disaffected troops was Ahmed Arabi Bey. Like many another who has moulded the destinies of kingdoms and peoples in the East, Arabi was born in the humblest surroundings. His parents were fellahin, who toiled in the wheat-fields of Lower Egypt by day, and slept by night in a squalid hut, built of mud and straw. We may suppose that Arabi's boyhood did not differ materially from that of others of his class. He grew, however, to a stature and strength that made him noticeable among his fellows; and in his earliest manhood he was drafted into the military service of Said; for the latter, like the great king of Prussia, loved a man of fine form. But, like that king, he also had a temper that sometimes got the better of his love, and at one of those times he had Arabi, for some slight fault, publicly bastinadoed and dismissed from the army. The latter now entered the university at Cairo, where he devoted himself to the fanatical studies enjoined by his religion and won for himself a reputation for learning, piety, and good morals. Loring Pasha, who knew him at that time, writes :

He was a fanatic in his close attention to the duties of his religion, rigidly following its superstitious customs, never neglecting his numerous prayers and ablutions, or his attendance at the mosque. Intimate with the sheiks and ulemas, he was always looked upon as a pillar of the faith.[1]

Upon Ismail's accession to the throne, Arabi reentered the army, where the influence of his studies brought him into prominence. Soon afterward he married the daughter of a nurse to one of the princes, and this connection gave him some acquaintance with royal affairs. But his power and popularity really had their beginning in a secret society that was organized in Cairo after the close of the Abyssinian campaign, in which Arabi had held the rank of lieutenant-colonel. His chief coadjutor in the formation of this society was Ali Pasha, and their object was to encourage a feeling of opposition among the fellah officers to the condition of affairs imposed on Egypt by the European control. Arabi had always been the friend of the fellahîn, from whom he sprang ; and it was the desire of his life to secure their rights.

[1] W. W. Loring, A Confederate Soldier in Egypt, p. 193.

When Tewfik ascended the throne, Arabi was made colonel, and his influence steadily increased. In 1881, therefore, the disaffected troops looked to him as their natural leader. His own experience under Said gave Arabi a sympathy for those officers who were removed without cause that Circassians and Turks might be given places, and he now became the champion of those who had been thus wronged. In February, Arabi and the other colonels demanded the dismissal of the minister of war, a Circassian who favored the Turks and hated the Arabs. As soon as the minister heard of the demand, he had Arabi and two colleagues arrested; but they were rescued from prison by Arabi's regiment and borne off in triumph. The Circassian, Osman, was removed, and Mahmûd Sami was appointed to his place. For some months, now, the distrust existing between the military party and the khédive increased. The colonels feared assassination, and the khédive a revolution. The rupture came on September 9, in the so-called "Insurrection of the Colonels." On the morning of that day Arabi submitted a document to the khédive, calling for the dismissal of the entire ministry, for the drafting of a constitution, and for the increase of the army to its limit, 18,000 men. On the afternoon of the same day, with 4,000 troops and eighteen cannon, the champion of the army marched to the palace to get the khédive's answer. Arabi intimated that, if the demands were not met, Tewfik's successor would be forthcoming. And still the khédive demurred ; but only for a time. He at length named a ministry—which, however, was unsatisfactory to Arabi. The latter demanded that the formation of the cabinet be left to Sherif Pasha. Sherif was second only to Nubar among Egyptian statesmen ; but he utterly lacked the latter's firmness of character. This was to Arabi's liking ; for he wanted not a master, but a slave. Sherif was, moreover, a good Mohammedan ; and he was therefore better liked by the people than Nubar, the Armenian. The khédive gave way to the inevitable, and on September 14 Sherif formed a new ministry.

The foreign Powers now awoke to the apparent danger of a still more formidable insurrection. As Mr. McCarthy rhetorically stated it :

> A wondering world began to ask whether Arabi Bey was the Cromwell of a great movement against an Egyptian Charles; the Garibaldi of a struggle for national liberty against a foreign rule; a scheming political adventurer, fighting for his own hand like Hal of the Wynd, or only a puppet, whose actions were guided by mysterious unseen strings.[1]

England was somewhat alarmed, but not to the extent of wishing to intervene herself. She wanted

[1] Justin McCarthy, M.P., England Under Gladstone, ch. xiii.

Turkey to send troops to Egypt to overawe the spirit of insurrection. But France would not consent to any kind of Turkish intervention. The sultan, however, was not to be baffled. The wily Abdul Hamid did not propose to let Egypt drift away from his suzerainty again to the length that it had under Ismail. He may not have had any determined policy. If he had, we are certainly ignorant of it. We simply know that he kept a jealous guard of his authority. From this time on there were intimations of mysterious signs of secret correspondence, first between the sultan and the khédive, and afterward between the sultan and Arabi; but the signs were almost never supplemented with proofs. Abdul Hamid did, however, take some steps openly that indicated a considerable degree of independence. He announced on September 20 that he had decided to send an emissary to Cairo. Both France and England protested; but, notwithstanding this, he dispatched two emissaries, October 3. Two days after this Lord Granville, the English minister of foreign affairs, proposed to M. St. Hilaire, who held the same portfolio for France, that the khédive be advised to receive the envoys, but "firmly to oppose any interference on their part in the internal administration of Egypt."[1] A joint note to this effect was sent to the khédive.

[1] Quoted from William Stone, M. A., Shall We Annex Egypt?

No sooner had the envoys arrived in Egypt than the feeling against the unbelievers began to show itself more openly. It is thought that the sultan sent secret messages to encourage a show of bitterness on the part of the students of the university of Cairo.[1] The foreign population became alarmed at the evidences of hatred and hostility. To reassure them, and to protect them if necessary, an English and a French vessel were sent at once to Alexandria. This move naturally excited the disapproval of the sultan; but Lord Granville said, through the English ambassador at Constantinople, that the warships must remain at Alexandria so long as the envoys remained in Egypt. The sultan hastily decided, therefore, to recall the envoys, and they left Egypt on October 19. Though their stay had been short, they had succeeded in fomenting the ill-feeling against England.

It was known that France was occupied with the new acquisition of Tunis, and all attention was turned to England with fear that she was bent on

[1] This great university has always been the hot-bed of Moslem fanaticism. When I arrived in Egypt, two months after the emissaries had been recalled, it was considered almost dangerous for foreigners to visit the university. A party of us went, however, and suffered no other indignity than hisses from the students whenever our faces were turned away. Some friends of mine were less fortunate in their visit a few weeks later. Not only were they hissed, but missiles were thrown at them, and they were actually set upon and driven from the place. The insult was prompted by the feeling that found vent a few months later in the massacre of Alexandria.

annexation. To allay this fear it became necessary for the British government, in November, to instruct Sir Edward Malet, her consular representative in Egypt, to assure the khédive's government that the British policy was opposed to intervention and foreign aggrandizement, and would not favor the separation of Egypt from Turkey, nor contend for more than the fulfillment of the sultan's firmans as already promulgated. It was declared, however, that this policy would not be maintained if disorders became prevalent. This was a firm note for Mr. Gladstone's government, which had not sought a control in the affairs of Egypt, but had been compelled, rather, by the circumstance of governmental inheritance, to accept what Disraeli bequeathed. The note had the effect of averting for a time the dread of British occupation. The feeling of security was still further increased by a joint letter addressed to the khédive by Lord Granville and M. Léon Gambetta, who had been called to the presidency of the French cabinet, November 14. Its purpose was less to calm the nationalists than to strengthen the khédive's government against the military party. The letter declared that England and France considered the maintenance of the khédive's power the sole guaranty of the present and future welfare of Egypt.

Soon after this, when all was apparently quiet in Egypt, I visited that country, and was privileged to have an interview with the Khédive, January 2, 1882, in which he dwelt at some length upon the reforms he was endeavoring to introduce. He desired and was aiming at three great reforms, religious, political, and educational. On the last he rightly laid the greatest stress.

For [said the khédive] while the people remain ignorant, reform in any direction is impossible; but let learning be spread among the people and throughout the land, and political and religious reform will follow as a natural consequence in the path of educational advancement. For this reason I am devoting my greatest energies to the spread of learning. The people must know more than the Koran; they must know geography and arithmetic and algebra and the sciences and the modern languages. All these pursuits and studies are now being advanced; schools are being founded in all the large towns of Egypt, both Upper and Lower, and now the numbers have increased from the ten or fifteen thousand I found on my accession to between eighty and ninety thousand students. My own boys attend the common schools; and, though princes to the world, they are there boys with the other boys and stand upon no different footing. Out of my own purse I have given fifteen thousand pounds a year to the schools since I came to the throne. Often, too, I go to the schools myself, and, if I say anything, I point to the United States for an example. I say that its greatness is due to the education of the people, to their enterprise, to their liberty of speech and freedom of thought; and I urge my people to become likewise educated, free, and great. Another reform that I am about to introduce is the education of women. Heretofore they have always been ignorant, more like slaves and animals than free women ; but now they, too, shall have their schools, and, being educated, they can be better mothers to their sons, the coming children of a new Egypt. Soon, now, one of these schools will be opened in Cairo, and I shall send there my own little daughter and the daughters of the nobility of Egypt, and then the others will come. The women of enlightened countries are on an equal footing with the men, and they must be here also ; and therefore they must be educated.

When travelers come here, I do not wish them to look upon us as barbarians, but as the most enlightened country of the Orient. We have been barbarous in some things ; but of these I wish to remove the last vestige, and I have already abolished some of the most atrocious practices of our religion. Last year I put an end to that barbarous ceremony of the Dosseh. Before then it was the custom, when the yearly pilgrims had returned from Mecca bearing the holy carpet, to have a great ceremony, most revolting and barbarous. One hundred men would lie prostrate at the door of the mosque, with head toward Mecca, and over their bodies would ride upon a horse the sheikh of the mosque. Always from eighteen to twenty of this hundred were killed under the feet of the horse. Europeans used to go in crowds to see this spectacle, and then call it barbarous. It is true, it was barbarous, and was without authority from the Bible, the Koran, or the Prophet ; and so I abolished it. People said a revolution would follow ; but we are better for the change.

Another change that I am working for is to make my

people content with one wife. I have but one myself, while my predecessor (my father) had many. I set the example I wish my people to follow; for, thank God, I make my own personal desire second to the welfare of Egypt and my people. When the people tell me the Koran says a man may have four wives, I tell them to read further on in the same book, where it says that the man who is content with one wife will lead a better, purer, and happier life. As it is now, family happiness is impossible. The children of one mother are jealous of those of another, and the man cannot be the same husband to four wives that he would be to one. The man and woman must be equal, and live their lives for each other and their children. And this, I say, is not inconsistent with, but the better interpretation of, our religion.

Further, I desire to make my people liberal in regard to religious beliefs and respectful towards Christians, Jews, and Mussulmans alike. They must not call the Christian the Devil, as they have heretofore; but must respect if they do not believe. I myself am a Mussulman. I go to the mosque once a week; for although my father did not do so before me, I nevertheless said, when I came into power, that I would respect my religion and live up to its teachings. But I encourage all religions. Here, in Cairo, I gave land on which to build a Protestant mission, where the young might be instructed; also other land on which to build a hospital, open to people of all religions; and just within a few days I have given land in Upper Egypt for the erection of another Protestant mission. All this I do without changing my own religion or asking others to change theirs. In fact, when a person wrote me the other day that he would like to change his religion for mine, I replied: Follow the teachings of your own religion and you will be good without any change.

It is difficult [the khedive went on, with a perceptible sadness in his voice] for me to do all that I would like to, or give my people all that I desire while other Powers have their hands in my pockets. Still, I have decreased the royal expenses greatly since I ascended the throne. My allowance is half a million dollars, and even out of this I give considerable. My father before me spent between ten and fifteen millions yearly in supporting his five or six hundred women and a palace and household that rivaled the Vatican for size. But I have great hopes for Egypt, and shall live and work for her prosperity.[1]

It will be admitted that these are views of an enlightened ruler, even though subsequent events may have proved him a weak one. The khédive's prime minister, Sherif Pasha, said at the same time:

Give us time for our reforms; let us have ten years of peaceful toiling, and Europe will be astonished at the vitality of a long-suffering nation, at the prosperity and wealth, the progress and rapid development of a country so long misgoverned, and for ages kept in ignorance and in the bondage of servitude.[2]

But there were so many disturbing elements in the condition of affairs in Egypt that the dream of "years of peaceful toiling" was as vain as it was impossible of realization.

---

[1] These utterances of the khédive were published in an article of mine in *The Independent*, February 2, 1882.

[2] Quoted from The Belgium of the East, p. 138.

V.

EGYPT FOR THE EGYPTIANS.

JANUARY 4, 1882, Arabi Bey was taken into the cabinet as assistant minister of war. Just before this the chamber of notables, strongly representative of the national party, had convened on the summons of Sherif Pasha. Sherif at once proposed a parliamentary reorganization, wishing to introduce the principle of ministerial responsibility, and gave the notables full constitutional prerogatives. They were to be no longer the mere consultative body that Ismail organized with his false show of reform. The notables had outgrown their former pious regard for the will of the khédive, and were not only willing to accept all that Sherif offered, but demanded in addition that the budget be submitted to them. This met with a quick opposition on the part of the comptrollers-general. The two Powers vetoed, January 7, the demand for constitutional government. Arabi and the nationalists were incensed. They longed for constitutional liberty and knew not that it appears only as the result of a slow internal growth, of which the germ had as yet barely taken root in Egypt. Outside of the Copts, the Christian Syrians, and the merchants of Cairo and Alexandria, there were few men in Egypt who had the faintest conception of what was meant by constitutional liberty. The Porte, however, not to neglect an opportunity to show its suzerainty, protested against the veto and appealed to the other Powers. Gambetta was eager to make the most of the complications, and proposed to England that they should dispatch a joint expedition to Egypt to re-establish order. England refused, and Gambetta's aggressiveness was cut short by the defeat of his ministry. He was succeeded by de Freycinet, whose policy was diametrically opposed to Gambetta's. The new minister was for non-interference. He replaced the zealous de Blignières by M. Bredif, thus giving England's representative in the control the predominance that goes with seniority.

While now the western Powers were occupied with diplomatic negotiations with the Porte, the chamber of notables submitted an alternative to Sherif Pasha: either he must accept their constitutional demands or resign from the ministry. He resigned, and Mahmûd Barûdi formed a new cabinet with Arabi Bey as minister of war and marine. The military party now took the lead.

Arabi and six other colonels were promoted to the rank of general, with the title of pasha. Some five hundred promotions were made during three months. At the same time many European clerks were dismissed from their offices. Arabi's popularity, meanwhile, was steadily increasing. In April he claimed to have discovered a plot to assassinate himself and other generals. Some fifty officers, many of them the still unpopular Circassians, and all of them believed to be loyal to the khédive, were arrested and tried by court-martial, and forty were sentenced to be banished for life to the White Nile—a sentence considered equivalent to death. This produced an agitation. The foreign consuls protested; the sultan was furious that the Circassians whom he had himself decorated with favors should be thus dishonored; and the khédive refused to give the sentence his signature. Finally, however, he commuted the sentence to exile from Egypt. But this 'displeased his nationalist ministry, who, on the 14th of May, convoked the chamber of notables without the consent of the khédive. The notables, however, refused to sit. At this juncture England and France, who had reconciled their differences, gave notice to the Powers that they were about to send a joint fleet to Alexandria to uphold the authority of the khédive and preserve the *status quo.* And the sultan, who slyly sought to ride on the crest of every wave, sent a note to the Egyptian ministry, chiding them for summoning the chamber unconstitutionally and rebuking them for their threat to oppose with force the landing of Turkish troops in Egypt. This was considered by the Powers an irregular communication on the part of the Porte. But the wily sultan was to be charged with still more irregular notes. His alleged secret correspondence from this time on is believed to have concealed many plots and intrigues.

On the 20th of May the united English and French squadrons appeared in the harbor of Alexandria. Five days later the English and French consuls demanded the dismissal of the ministry and the expatriation of Arabi. The ministers forthwith handed in their resignations; but Arabi declared that he would remain at the head of the army. In the meantime the fortifications about Alexandria were increased and the harbor was put in a state of defence. The guards at Cairo swore to oppose with force any foreign intervention; and the sheikhs and Bedawin of the desert promised their support against European, but not against Turkish, intervention. Lord Dufferin, the English ambassador at Constantinople, naïvely informed the sultan that, as the Porte's authority had never been called into question, it would not be necessary for Turkish troops to co-operate to quell the fractious spirit; England and France would be quite equal to the task. The poor khédive, from the day he dismissed the ministry, was beset with trials and torments. He could not form a new ministry, and the utmost influence was brought to bear to force him to reinstate Arabi as minister of war. The commanders of the Alexandria fortification said they would obey the orders of no one but Arabi. Notables, sheikhs, ulemas, officers, urged and even demanded the reinstatement. At length Tewfik was forced to give way. The sultan telegraphed that he would send a commissioner to Egypt to investigate the troubles. France objected strenuously to his coming, but England and the other Powers thought that he might avert the impending danger. England, however, continued to oppose any military expedition from Turkey. De Freycinet felt that France had been left in the lurch, and proposed that a conference of all the Powers be held at Constantinople to settle the Egyptian question definitely. But in the meantime the sultan had dispatched Dervish Pasha to Egypt to lend support, as he announced, to the khédive.

The commissioner arrived on the 8th of June. His presence had no quieting effect. Arabi was the only minister who had been appointed; and he was, in fact, the hero and the autocrat of the hour.

But, through the influence of Dervish, a ministry was formed favorable to the khédive, with Ragheb as president. It was, however, powerless to still the tumult of passion that had been aroused in Egypt during the past few months. Hatred of the Christians was shouted through the streets.[1] The people who had cowered before the kûrbash during all the woes of Ismail's reign, who had seen the wealth of the Nile valley melt away before their eyes year after year, who had abjectly begged for *backsheesh* from every stranger in their land, now sprang to a position of independence and defiance. Fanaticism was burning to its utmost intensity. It became a flame of fury on the 11th of June, in the massacre at Alexandria.

Just what the immediate cause of that outbreak was, is a disputed point. It is claimed, on the one hand, that it began by a Maltese stabbing an Arab; and, on the other, that the massacre was preconcerted, being countenanced by Arabi himself. Colonel Long, who was in Cairo at the time, says [2] that a secret council was held in that city on the evening before the massacre, which Arabi and several of the notables attended. One of the number, who had openly preached the duty of massacre in the mosques of Alexandria, arrived in that city before the hour of the slaughter. The troops at Alexandria, who

[1] Col. Chaillé Long, The Three Prophets, p. 119. [2] *Ibid.*, p. 120.

had proclaimed that they would obey the orders of no one but Arabi, turned their bayonets against the Europeans and aided the Arabs in the massacre. The police joined the same mad throng. These facts would seem to point toward complicity on the part of Arabi. The massacre was as horrible in its way as the massacre of the memlûks in 1811, or the Syrian massacre of 1860. The Oriental is frenzied at the sight of blood and impelled to the most atrocious crimes. His fury does not spend itself; it is only checked when the opportunity of bloodshed is exhausted or some force interposed. The Maltese, the Greeks, and other Europeans banded together and offered, at last, an effectual resistance; but not before about a hundred of their number had been butchered, and some five hundred Arabs had been killed.

Abuse was heaped upon the English and French admirals, who had offered no assistance to the Europeans of Alexandria, although they had witnessed the outrages and had sufficient force on the ships, within sight, to quell the disturbance. Their boats were ready to land the marines, but the admirals could not act without orders from their governments. So they said, at least; but they might as well have claimed that they should not take in sail at the approach of a hurricane except by governmental sanction. As Colonel Long says: "It is difficult to understand the hesitancy of an officer to assume responsibility, however great, in the presence of a great crime like this committed against humanity."[1]

The massacre created, naturally, a panic among the Europeans in Egypt. They fled from Cairo to Alexandria, and from Alexandria they took passage in any craft that would bear them from the scene of crime and the seat of danger. It was a stampede for life, with no thought of the property forsaken. The khédive, accompanied by Dervish Pasha, went to Alexandria, June 13, to endeavor to restore quiet by his presence. He formed a new ministry at the dictation of the German and Austrian consuls, June 16, giving Arabi his old place as minister of war, and retaining Ragheb as president of the council. But England and France refused to recognize the ministry. The khédive was in despair. His departure from Cairo had left Arabi virtual ruler there. The latter was at the high tide of his power. The sultan, immediately after the massacre, had conferred a great honor upon him by investing him with the order of the Medjidieh. Dervish Pasha, the sultan's representative, was believed to be working in his behalf, and to be fomenting rebellion. Arabi said himself when, months later, his power was gone:

The Sultan, the real sovereign of this country, also sided with us and loaded us with marks of his approba-

[1] The Three Prophets, p. 129.

tion. His representative concurred in our resistance, and his trusted officers exhorted us to defend the country from what they termed the rapacity of England. The opening acts of the war were carried on in his name.[1]

So far back as February, the chaplain to the sultan had written to Arabi: " In a special and secret manner I may tell you that the Sultan has no confidence in Ismail, Halim, or Tewfik. . . . His Majesty has expressed his full confidence in you."[2] During the flight of the Europeans, Arabi was sounding his cry of " Egypt for the Egyptians," and was exercising the utmost activity possible in military preparations. The warlike spirit had spread throughout the country, and recruits and money were pouring in. Work on the fortifications at Alexandria was pushed with renewed vigor.

Meanwhile the conference of Powers had met at Constantinople, June 23; but nothing had been accomplished. The Porte would not commit itself to policy or to action. It is probable, however, that it contemplated the restoration of all its old power in Egypt. England, at all events, feared this. The possibility of such a thing was a menace to the Indian empire. While, therefore, the conference was slowly seeking a solution of difficulties,

[1] Ahmed Arabi, Instructions to my Counsel, in *The Nineteenth Century*, December, 1882.
[2] Quoted from Arabi's papers in Broadley's How We Defended Arabi, pp. 169 and 170.

England resolved to take decisive action; not so much, as has been held by some, to mete out punishment for the Alexandrian massacre as to protect her interests in Egypt and the farther East. But, whatever her motives, she acted in the service of the world's civilization when she set her face against the restoration of the sultan's power in Egypt.

On the 6th of July, Sir Beauchamp Seymour, the admiral of the British fleet at Alexandria, protested against the continued work on the fortifications about the harbor, and announced to the military governor, Tûlba, that unless the work ceased he would open fire upon the fortresses. Tûlba replied that the admiral's assertions as to the work of fortifying were unfounded. But electric lights from the British vessels discovered the Egyptian soldiers hard at work by night. July 10, Admiral Seymour sent a second message:

> I shall carry out the intention expressed to you in my letter of the 6th inst., at sunrise to-morrow, the 11th inst., unless, previous to that hour, you shall have temporarily surrendered to me, for the purpose of disarming the batteries on the isthmus of Ras-el-Tin and the southern shore of the harbor of Alexandria.

The khédive's prime minister replied to this, refusing to comply with the admiral's demands; whereupon the latter sent a brief message containing the implication that his threat would be carried out. These messages had not been exchanged without creating great alarm among the Europeans who still remained in Egypt. The consuls appealed to the admiral for delay and sought to mediate, and the Porte, through its London ambassador, demanded that the bombardment be interdicted; but the admiral's determination remained unaltered. Endeavors were now made to put all remaining foreigners on shipboard. Many had lingered in Cairo, loth to leave their posts or their property. The notice given them was short —so short that Admiral Seymour has been bitterly blamed for his haste.[1] The impending bombardment, it was known, would be avenged on any unfortunate foreigners who might thereafter fall into Arab hands.

Late on the afternoon of July 10, all the vessels in the Alexandrian harbor, except the British fleet, weighed anchor and passed out to sea, their decks swarming with refugees of many nationalities. The French fleet was among the departing ships. If a Gambetta had been premier of the French government, Admiral Conrad would have remained. He would have insisted upon joint action or joint inaction. But de Freycinet was weak. After see-

[1] *Vide* Stone Pasha's Introduction to Fanny Stone's Diary, in *The Century Magazine*, June, 1884.

ing the disfavor with which France had suffered intervention in Tunis, he feared to sanction intervention in Egypt. And so Admiral Conrad and his fleet sailed away; and France, as the sequel has shown, passed from a controlling power in Egypt.

The story of the bombardment of Alexandria, from a military point of view, is best told from the official reports [1] of Admiral Seymour. He wrote the following from his flagship *Invincible*, July 20:

At 7 A.M., on the 11th, I signalled from the *Invincible* to the *Alexandria* to fire a shell into the recently armed earthworks, termed the Hospital Battery, and followed this by a general signal to the fleet, "Attack the enemy's batteries!" when immediate action ensued between all the ships in the positions assigned to them, and the whole of the forts commanding the entrance to the harbor of Alexandria. A steady fire was maintained on all sides until 10.30 A.M., when the *Sultan*, *Superb*, and *Alexandria*, which had been hitherto under way, anchored off the Light-House Fort, and by their well-directed fire, assisted by that of the *Inflexible*, which weighed and joined them at 12.30 P.M., succeeded in silencing most of the guns in the forts on Ras-el-Tin; still some heavy guns in Fort Ada kept up a desultory fire. About 1.30 P.M., a shell from the *Superb*, whose practice in the afternoon was very

[1] These official reports, as well as detailed descriptions of the defences of Alexandria and of the attacking fleet, and statements of the effect of the fight upon ships and fortifications, are given by Lieutenant-Commander Casper F. Goodrich, of the U. S. Navy, in his Report of the British Naval and Military Operations in Egypt.

good, blew up the magazine and caused the retreat of the remaining garrison. These ships then directed their attention to Fort Pharos, which was silenced with the assistance of the *Temeraire*, which joined them at 2.30 P.M., when a shot from the *Inflexible* dismounted one of the heavy guns. The Hospital Battery was well fought throughout; and, although silenced for a time by a shell from the *Inflexible*, it was not until 5 P.M. that the artillerymen were compelled to retire from their guns by the fire of the off-shore squadron and the *Inflexible*. The *Invincible*, with my flag, supported by the *Penelope*, both ships being at anchor, the latter on one occasion shifting berth, and assisted by the *Monarch*, under way inside the reefs, as well as by the *Inflexible* and *Temeraire* in the Boghaz and Corvette Channels, succeeded, after an engagement of some hours, in silencing and partially destroying the batteries and lines of Mex. Fort Marsa-el-Khanat was destroyed by the explosion of the magazine after half an hour's action with the *Monarch*.

About 2 P.M., seeing that the gunners of the western lower battery of Mex had abandoned their guns, and that the supporters had probably retired to the citadel, I called in the gun-vessels and gun-boats, and under cover of their fire landed a party of twelve volunteers, under the command of Lieut. B. R. Bradford, of the *Invincible*, accompanied by Lieut. Richard Poore, of that ship, . . . [and three others] . . . who got on shore through the surf, and destroyed, with charges of gun-cotton, two 10-inch M. L. R. guns, and spiked six smooth-bore guns in the right-hand water battery at Mex, and returned without a casualty beyond the loss of one of their boats (*Bittern's* dingy) on the rocks. This was a hazardous operation very well carried out. Previous to this, after the action had become general, Commander Lord Charles Beresford, of the *Condor*, stationed as repeating ship, seeing the accuracy with which two 10-inch rifled guns in Fort Marabout were playing upon the ships engaged off Fort Mex, steamed up to within range of his 7-inch 90 cwt. gun, and by his excellent practice soon drew off the fire. I then ordered him to be supported by the *Beacon*, *Bittern*, *Cygnet*, and *Decoy*, the *Cygnet* having been engaged with the Ras-el-Tin forts during the early part of the day. I am happy to say, during the action, no casualties happened to those vessels, owing, in a great measure, to the able manner in which they were manœuvred, and their light draught enabling them to take up their positions on the weakest point of the batteries. The action generally terminated successfully at 5.30 P.M., when the ships anchored for the night.

The force opposed to us would have been more formidable had every gun mounted on the line of works been brought into action; but in the Ras-el-Tin batteries, few of the large smooth-bores, and fewer still of the French 36-pounders, bought in the time of Mehemet Ali, were manned, the Egyptians preferring to use the English 10-inch, 9-inch, 8-inch, and smaller muzzle-loading rifled guns. These guns are precisely the same as those which her Majesty's ships carry, and no better muzzle-loading guns can be found. They were abundantly, even lavishly, supplied with projectiles of the latest description, chilled shot, and the sighting of the guns was excellent. The same may be said of the guns in the Mex Lines, excepting that in them the 36-pounders were more used, and that one, if not two, 15-inch smooth-bores were brought into action, in addition to the 10-inch, 9-inch, and smaller M. L. R. guns fired. Fort Marabout brought two 10-inch M. L. R. guns into action at long range, shell after shell of which came up toward the in-shore squadron in an excellent line, falling from ten to thirty yards short. Not one shell from the guns in the southern batteries burst on board her Majesty's ships during the day.

Though the Arabs' shells failed, their other shot took effect. The *Alexandria* was struck twenty-five times, and the *Invincible* was pierced by six shots. The shells from the ships burst, many of them, over or in the city, destroying much property. The English loss for the day was six killed and twenty-seven wounded. The Arab loss was much greater. At least one hundred and fifty men in the forts were killed ; but trustworthy information as to their casualties is wanting. The Arabs stood by their guns with an undreamed-of courage ; for the forts were not silenced till the gunners had been killed. On the 12th of July the firing was resumed. Admiral Seymour said, in his dispatch :

On the morning of the 12th I ordered the *Temeraire* and *Inflexible* to engage Fort Pharos, and after two or three shots had been fired a flag of truce was hoisted on Fort Ras-el-Tin, and I then sent my flag lieutenant, the Honorable Hedworth Lambton, in to discover the reason, and, from his report, there is no doubt it was simply a ruse to gain time ; and, as negotiations failed, my demand being to surrender the batteries commanding the Boghaz Channel, one shot was fired into the Mex Barracks Battery earthwork, when a flag of truce was again hoisted. I then sent Lieutenant and Commander Morrison into the harbor, in the *Helicon*, and on his going on board the khédive's yacht, the *Mahrussa*, he found she had been deserted, and he reported, on his return after dark, his belief that the town had been evacuated.

Such, indeed, was the fact. Arabi had gone, but the khédive had remained. The khédive had presided at a cabinet council, held at Ras-el-Tin, on the morning of the 10th, and had given his sanction to the proposed defence of the city. That evening, accompanied by Dervish Pasha and his immediate household, he retired to the palace of Ramleh, where he remained during the bombardment. On the afternoon of the 12th he sent to Admiral Seymour, imploring his protection. Arabi claimed that by this act the khédive basely deserted his people. But Tewfik feared for his life. A band of soldiers had sought entrance to the palace, asserting that they had Arabi's instructions to murder the khédive. Arabi is said to have countermanded this order and to have stationed a guard about the palace, when he determined to evacuate the city. Another story states that Tewfik bought his life with bribes and orders of distinction. At all events the trembling Tewfik remained at Ramleh while Arabi withdrew his forces and his followers along the Mahmûdieh canal.

And now the fair city of Alexandria became such a scene of pillage, massacre, and wanton destruction as to make the world shudder. It was the old tale of horrors. Houses were plundered and burned; the European quarter, including the stately buildings surrounding the Great Square of Mehemet Ali, was sacked and left a heap of smoldering ruins; and more than two thousand Europeans, for the most part Levantines, were massacred with all the cruelty of oriental fanaticism. This was on the afternoon of the 12th. It was the second massacre that had occurred under the very eyes of the British fleet. The admiral's failure to prevent it has been called unfortunate by some and criminal by others. It seems to have been wholly without excuse. The most plausible palliation of the neglect is found in Lieutenant-Commander Goodrich's "Report," but even that carries its blame. He says (page 75):

A few hundred men could have seized and held the place on July 12th, so great was the fear on the part of the Egyptians, both soldiers and citizens, caused by the bombardment—a fear not known, at the time, to the British Commander-in-chief. In consequence of the lack of information, this memorable battle was followed by one of the most shocking, wanton, and deplorable catastrophes of the century.

The blue-jackets were landed on the 13th, and

cleared the way before them with a Gatling gun. The next day, more ships having arrived, a sufficient force was landed to take possession of the entire city. The khédive was escorted back to Ras-el-Tin from Ramleh, and given a strong guard. Summary justice was dealt out to all hostile Arabs who had been captured in the city. In short, English intervention was followed by English occupation.

The bombardment of Alexandria had defined clearly the respective positions of Arabi and the khédive toward Egypt and the Egyptian people. The soldiers and the sympathy of the land were with Arabi. His cry was, "Egypt for the Egyptians," and these words embodied everything that was held dear and sacred by the people. The khédive was not only weak in the eyes of his people, but he was regarded as the tool of England. He had deserted his soldiers and fallen on his knees to beg the protection of unbelievers. From the moment the first shot was fired upon Alexandria, Arabi was the real ruler of the people. But England could never suffer Egypt to exist solely "for the Egyptians." With France, she had placed Tewfik on the throne to protect the interests of her bondholders, and to secure her power in and over the country alongside of which flowed the chiefest artery of her commercial life. Her duty and her interest compelled the re-establishment of Tewfik's power. He was the nominal ruler, and must once more be made so in fact. If Arabi refused to end his preparations for war at the bidding of the khédive, and persisted in opposing the defenders of the khédive, then he was a rebel and the leader of rebellion, and he must be compelled by force to submit. Such was the reasoning that led England to play the role of the khédive's defender and to prepare for a war in Egypt.

The conference at Constantinople was stirred by the news of the bombardment of Alexandria. It presented a note to the Porte, July 15, requesting the dispatch of Turkish troops to restore the *status quo* in Egypt. But the sultan had no idea of taking the part of the Christian in what all Islam regarded as a contest between the Moslem and the unbeliever. Arabi had called himself the defender of the faith. He and his followers were the soldiers of the Prophet. The ulemas and dignitaries of the mosques of Stambûl advised the sultan not to risk his caliphate by opposing the heroes of the Mohammedan faith. And so Abdul-Hamid deliberated and delayed. France was uneasy at the prospect of war, and Gambetta, now the leader of the opposition, was furious at the prospect of being out of the row. He appealed to the French chamber to insist upon dual intervention, but in vain. Even the timid de Freycinet went farther than the chamber would sanction. He proposed to confine operations to the protection of the Suez canal, and applied for a supplementary credit in order to undertake the necessary military preparations. But the credit was denied, and he resigned, July 24. A ministry with a policy of positive inactivity was formed by M. Duclerc. Contrasted to the strange inertness of France was the attempt at interference on the part of Russia, Austria, and Italy. Russia would have given Egypt to England if she could have won the Bosphorus as an offset; but Prince Bismarck did not approve of the contemplated annexation by Russia, and his power over Austria and Italy was such as to enable him to frustrate the plan. The sultan appealed to Bismarck to support the Porte against England as well; but this the German chancellor declined to do, telling the sultan that he must yield to the inevitable in Egypt. And thus the diplomatic contest was left to the chief combatants, England and Turkey.

In Egypt, the khédive had been prevailed upon, after some demur, to proclaim Arabi a rebel and discharge him from his cabinet. Arabi had issued a counter-proclamation, on the same day, declaring Tewfik a traitor to his people and his religion. Having received the news of the khédive's proclamation, Lord Dufferin, the British ambassador at

Constantinople, announced to the conference that England was about to send an expedition to Egypt to suppress the rebellion and to restore the authority of the khédive. Thereupon the sultan declared that he had decided to send a Turkish expedition. Lord Dufferin feigned to accept the sultan's co-operation, but demanded that the Porte, as a preliminary step, should declare Arabi a rebel. Again the sultan was confronted with the danger of incurring the wrath of the Moslem world. He could not declare Arabi a rebel. He was manifestly in an uncomfortable position. His sympathies were with Arabi. But if he fought, he must fight against him; for he could not oppose England; and if he kept out of the fray, he must suffer the humiliation of seeing a foreign force settle the affairs of his suzerainty. He was between two fires. In his desperation he sent a force of three thousand men to Suda bay with orders to hold themselves in readiness to enter Egypt at a moment's notice. Lord Dufferin now submitted a proposal for co-operation, naming the following conditions :

1. That the Turkish contingent should be restricted to 5,000 men. 2. That it should land at Abûkir, Damietta, or Rosetta. 3. That its movements and operations should be regulated by a previous agreement between the English and Turkish commanders. 4. That a Turkish military commissioner should be attached to the English head-

quarters and an English commissioner to the Turkish headquarters; and, 5. That the English and Turkish troops should evacuate Egypt simultaneously.'

The representatives of the Porte in the conference would not accept these conditions, wishing any Turkish expedition to act independently of England. In the meantine, however, the English expedition had arrived in Egypt and was proceeding to crush the rebellion, regardless of the diplomatic delays and bickerings at Constantinople.

[1] Quoted from Appleton's *Annual Cyclopædia* for 1882, p. 250.

VI.

ARABI'S REBELLION AND THE REFORMS THAT
FOLLOWED.

FOR a month after the bombardment, the British army at Alexandria was satisfied simply to hold its position. Lieutenant-Commander Goodrich describes the role it played during this time as "of a negative character, in the main consisting in an efficient if passive defence of the city against the Egyptians encamped and intrenched at King Osman and Kafr Dowar."[1] Several sorties, however, were made on the armed railway trains; but there was scarcely an engagement worthy the name. On the 21st of July an army corps, under the command of General Sir Garnet Wolseley, had been ordered to Egypt, and pending his arrival the army of occupation preserved, for the most part, an attitude of defence, though making an occasional reconnoissance. On the 28th of July the British Parliament formally recognized the preparations for war by a vote of two million three hundred

[1] Report, p. 87.

thousand pounds for the expense of the expedition. It was not until the 15th of August that Sir Garnet Wolseley arrived with his force[1] in Egypt. The English at that time held only two points, Alexandria and Suez, while the entire Egyptian interior, as well as Port Said and Ismailia, were held by Arabi, whose force, it was estimated, now amounted to about 70,000 men, of whom at least 50,000 were regulars.

The objective point of General Wolseley's expedition to crush Arabi was, of course, the city of Cairo. There were two ways of approaching that city, one from Alexandria, through the Delta, and the other from the Suez canal. There were many objections to the former route. The Delta was intersected by a net-work of canals, dikes, ditches, and railways, all of which were in Arabi's hands and made the region easily defensible. In fact, the banks of the canals and dikes were natural fortifications as they stood. On the other hand, the way from Ismailia, the central station on the Suez canal, to Cairo, was along an unobstructed and single railway route. Then, too, the desert by the latter route

---

[1] Lieutenant-Commander Goodrich (Report, p. 104) gives the following totals of the principal corps under General Wolseley's command: Infantry, 15,642 (officers and men); cavalry, 2,304; artillery, including siege trains, 2,435; engineers, 1,161; commissariat and transport corps, 1,298; army hospital corps, 313; army medical department, 429. The Indian contingent brought the total number of men up to about 35,000.

was comparatively free from the pestilential diseases of the Delta. Owing to the Sweet Water canal, the question of water presented no difficulties. There was, however, an obstacle to the choice of Ismailia as a base of operations; but it was a purely moral one, and was easily overcome or rather disregarded. The Suez canal was supposed to be neutral water. Count Ferdinand de Lesseps, the president of the Suez canal company, assured Arabi, whom he met at Ismailia after the opening of hostilities, that England would so regard it, and thus prevented Arabi from establishing Egyptian fortifications along the canal. But England felt no obligation to recognize any neutrality. De Freycinet's scheme to enforce the neutrality had cost him his premiership, and there was little force in the orders and threats of the president of the canal company. England, therefore, consulted simply her own interests, acting upon the principle, which is doubtless sound, that "the neutrality of any canal joining the waters of the Atlantic and Pacific oceans will be maintained, if at all, by the nation which can place and keep the strongest ships at each extremity."[1] In other words, General Wolseley decided to enter Cairo by way of the Suez canal and Ismailia.

But he kept his plan a profound secret. Admiral

[1] Stated thus in Goodrich's Report, p. 125.

Seymour alone knew his purpose. On the 18th of August, all the orders for an attack on Abûkir, where Arabi's force was concentrated, were issued, and concerning this plan rumors were purposely allowed to reach the newspaper correspondents. On the 19th, the transports moved eastward from Alexandria, as if to attack Abûkir; but under the cover of darkness that night, they were escorted on to Port Said, where they learned that the entire canal, owing to the preconcerted action of Admiral Seymour, was in the hands of the British. On the 21st, the troops met Sir Henry McPherson's Indian contingent at Ismailia. Two days were now consumed in rest and preparation. The Egyptians cut off the water supply, which came from the Delta by the Sweet Water canal, by damming the canal. A sortie to secure possession of the dam was therefore deemed necessary, and was successfully made on the 24th. Further advances were made, and on the 26th, Kassassin, a station of some importance on the canal and railway, was occupied. Here the British force was obliged to delay for two weeks, while organizing a hospital and a transport service. This gave Arabi opportunity to concentrate his forces at Zagazig and Tel-el-Kebir. But he knew it was for his interest to strike at once before the British transports could come up with the advance. He therefore made two attempts, one on August 28, and the other on September 9, to regain the position lost at Kassassin. But he failed [1] in both, though inflicting some loss upon his opponents.

On the 12th of September preparations were made by General Wolselev for a decisive battle.

[1] Arabi could not recognize defeat. His despatches to the ministry of war at Cairo concerning the engagement of September 9, are, to say the least, amusing. In one he said (*vide* Goodrich's Report, p. 144): "At sunrise the enemy came out with infantry, cavalry, and artillery, and firing began, and continued on both sides for about an hour. Then the Arabs charged like lions, displaying a courage and bravery which enabled them to drive back the enemy, who were much more numerous than ourselves. Then they followed the enemy, driving them until they had killed about 100 of them [the British official report says two], and dispersed the rest, driving them back into their tents. The Arabs captured their oxen, about 500 meters of torpedo-wire, and other military stores, and then returned to their posts victorious. This engagement, including the attack and the pursuit, lasted about six hours. . . . Thanks be to God, not one of the Arabs nor of the soldiers was wounded. Give this news to those under your administration." Three days after, he sent another despatch, with a different statement as to casualties: "I give you good news, which will cause you joy, and will delight each individual of the people—namely, that the engagement of Saturday (9th of September) was the most serious battle that has yet taken place between us and the English; for the force of both armies was very great, and the fighting lasted for twelve hours, with impetuosity and daring, while the cannonade and the discharge of musketry were unceasing, pouring down like rain on the field of battle. Still we lost only thirty-one men, martyrized, and 150 were slightly, not dangerously, wounded, according to the official returns presented by the various regiments with great exactness and precision. It had been thought that our casualties would have been double that number, owing to the seriousness of the engagement and its long duration. Moreover, from true observation, it has been proved to us that the number of the enemy killed and remaining on the field of battle is about 2,500, and their carts were insufficient for carrying off the wounded," *etc.*

He had become convinced [1] from daily reconnoissance and from the view obtained in the engagement of September 9, that the fortifications at Tel-el-Kebir were both extensive and formidable. Against an enemy so strongly intrenched, and whose force consisted of about 38,000 men and fifty-nine siege-guns, it would have been folly to advance across an open desert; and it was therefore decided to make the approach under cover of darkness. All possible precautions were taken to guard against alarm. Bugle calls and fires were prohibited after nightfall, and strict silence was enjoined. The camp was struck as noiselessly as possible, and at 1.30 on the morning of the 13th General Wolseley gave the order for the advance, his force consisting of about 11,000 infantry, 2,000 cavalrymen, and sixty field-guns. They had only the stars to guide them, but so accurately was the movement conducted that the leading brigades of each division reached the enemy's outposts within two minutes of each other.

The enemy [says General Wolseley] were completely surprised, and it was not until one or two of their advanced sentries fired their rifles that they realized our close proximity to their works. These were, however, very quickly lined with infantry, who opened a deafening musketry fire, and their guns came into action immediately. Our

[1] *Vide* his official report of the battle of Tel-el-Kebir, dated Cairo, September 16, 1882.

troops advanced steadily without firing a shot, in obedience to the orders they had received; and, when close to the works, went straight for them, charging with a ringing cheer.[1]

The intrenchments were not carried without a severe struggle. The Egyptians fought with a desperate courage, and hundreds of them were bayoneted at their posts. "More intelligence," declares Lieutenant-Commander Goodrich,[2] "and less downright cowardice in the upper grades might have converted these men into a formidable army." But what could the rank and file accomplish when "each officer knew that he would run, but hoped his *neighbor* would stay."[3] At the first shot Arabi and his second in command took horse and galloped to Belbeis, where they caught a train for Cairo. Most of the other officers, as the reports of killed and wounded show, did the same.

The Egyptians fired their first shot at 4.55 A.M., and at 6.45 the English had possession of Arabi's headquarters and the canal bridge. The British loss was 57 killed, 380 wounded, and 22 missing. The Egyptian army left about 2,000 dead in the fortifications. There is no report of the number of the Egyptian wounded; but it probably was not proportionate to the number killed; for, if rumor is to be trusted, the wounded were not spared by

[1] *Ibid.* [2] Goodrich's Report, p. 15. [3] *Ibid.*

the British saber and bayonet. There was, however, some excuse for the alleged cruelty on the part of the attacking troops. An Egyptian, like the wild beast of the jungle, gets an added ferocity and desperation with each wound. "So many cases are authenticated," says Lieutenant-Commander Goodrich,[1] "of the virulence displayed by the Egyptian wounded, that it is demonstrated, beyond question, that many of these fellows not only shot at the stretchermen engaged in carrying off the injured, but, in some cases, actually killed the very Englishmen who had stopped to give them water or to bind their wounds." The same author makes the following observations upon the battle from a military point of view:

In view of the decisiveness of the victory, comment appears unnecessary. It may be alleged that the mode of attack adopted was hazardous to the degree of imprudence; that no commander would dare to employ such tactics on European territory; that a night march of nine miles could only be followed by a properly disposed and immediate assault under circumstances so exceptional as to be providential. It must, however, be remembered that General Wolseley understood his enemy, knew his military habits and numbers, as well as the ground intervening; had a fairly good idea of his intrenchments, a just appreciation of his *morale*, a strong conviction as to the proper manner of engaging him, and confidence in the

[1] *Ibid.*

officers and men of his own command. What he would have done had the enemy been of a different character, is another question, whose consideration does not come within the province of this report. It seems a sufficient answer to such criticisms as are briefly referred to above, to remark that the means were adjusted to the end to be reached, and that the justification (if any be needed) of the risks incurred lies in the success which attended them —a success as rare as it was complete.¹

A proof of the completeness of the success was the entire dissipation of Arabi's army. Groups of soldiers, it is true, were scattered to different parts of Egypt; but the army organization was completely broken up with the battle of Tel-el-Kebir.

The movements that followed the decisive victory were promptly begun and most effectively executed. The best account is given in the words of General Wolseley's dispatch of September 16

The enemy were pursued to Zagazig, twenty-five miles from our camp at Kassassin, by the Indian Contingent, the leading detachment of which reached that place, under Major-General Sir H. Macpherson, V. C., a little after 4 P. M., and by the cavalry division, under General Lowe, to Belbeis, which was occupied in the evening. Major-General Lowe was ordered to push on with all possible speed to Cairo, as I was most anxious to save that city from the fate which befell Alexandria in July last.

These orders were ably carried out, General Lowe reach-

¹ Goodrich's Report, p. 158.

ing the great barracks of Abbassieh, just outside of Cairo, at 4.45 P. M., on the 14th instant. The cavalry marched sixty-five miles in these two days. The garrison of about 10,000 men, summoned by Lieutenant-Colonel H. Stewart, assistant adjutant-general to the cavalry division, to surrender, laid down their arms, and our troops took possession of the citadel. A message was sent to Arabi Pasha through the prefect of the city, calling upon him to surrender forthwith, which he did unconditionally. He was accompanied by Tûlba Pasha, who was also one of the leading rebels in arms against the Khédive.

The Guards, under His Royal Highness the Duke of Connaught, reached Cairo early on the 15th instant.

With an energy, as remarkable as it was praiseworthy, General Wolseley prevented the war ending with horrors [1] like those with which it began. Arabi's

[1] The death of the eminent oriental scholar, Professor Palmer, which occurred on August 12, 1882, was one of the horrible tragedies for which the Egyptian war was responsible. Justin McCarthy (England Under Gladstone, ch. xiii.) makes the following reference to the loss the world sustained in his death: "Professor Edward Palmer was one of those rare men who possess what appears to be an almost incredible facility for learning languages. He was well-nigh the ideal scholar, devoted to learning for learning's sake, yet never tainted by the faintest tinge of pedantry, pride, or affectation. The story of his life has been told by his close friend, attached admirer, and literary colleague, the well-known novelist, Mr. Walter Besant. It is a touching and thrilling record of marvellous accomplishments, of brilliant performance, of patient, determined struggle toward success, of success achieved, of honors won, of firm friendship, and a peaceful, happy home— and all ended by a sudden, terrible death in the Wady Sudr. In the summer of 1882, Professor Palmer agreed to go out for the Government to Egypt to prevent any alliance between Arabi and the Bedawîn tribes of the desert. It seems strange that so precious a life should have been risked on such an errand, though Professor Palmer's knowledge of the languages of the East was proverbial. It is not very surprising that, when he and his

revenge was forestalled by that rapid desert journey. Before leaving England, Wolseley had predicted that he would enter Cairo on the 16th of September; but with still a day to spare the feat was accomplished, and Arabi's rebellion was completely crushed.

England now stood alone. Victory had been won without the aid of France or the intervention of Turkey. In Constantinople negotiations regarding Turkish expeditions were still pending when Lord Dufferin received the news of Wolseley's success, and announced to the Porte that there was now no need of a Turkish force in Egypt, as the war was ended. France at once prepared to resume her share in the control; but England, having borne the sole burden of the war, did not propose now to share the influence her success had given her. And it was for the interest of Egypt that she should not. As in the campaign just

party were captured by hostile Arabs, their doom should be death. It is certain that short work would have been made of any emissary from Arabi who was caught attempting to interfere with the relations existing between some English general, and, say, an Indian regiment. We shall, perhaps, never exactly know the story of the tragedy near Nakl. It is certain, however, that Palmer and his companions were captured through the treachery of the Sheikh Meter Sofieh, who was their guide, and that Palmer, Captain Gill, and Lieutenant Charrington were shot. Some thirteen of the Arabs of the tribe that killed Palmer and his companions were afterward captured, brought to trial, and five of them were hanged at Zagazig on February 28, 1883. The remains of Palmer, Gill, and Charrington were recovered, carried to England, and interred in St. Paul's Church."

ended England had been able to achieve a quicker and more effectual success alone than would have been possible with a joint command of jealous Powers, so now, peace having been restored, a single supervision and direction promised a steadfastness to the government that could not have been effected under a re-establishment of the joint control. While there was a general agreement in England as to what other Powers should not do, there was a wide difference of opinion as to the individual course to be pursued by the British government. Lord Derby, who became colonial secretary soon after the end of the war, was in favor of withdrawing from Egypt altogether, and leaving the country to "stew in her own juice"; but the judgment that declared that anarchy in Egypt would mean injury to the world prevailed. Egypt could not stand alone; and Anglo-Saxon support, with its civilizing influences, was the best to be found.

England's first duty, after quiet was assured, was to send away all the British troops except a force of about 11,000 men, which it was deemed advisable to retain in Egypt until the khédive's authority was placed on a safe footing throughout the land. At the same time it was decided to reorganize the military establishment of Egypt, and Baker Pasha, an Englishman in the service of the sultan, was invited to superintend this work. The khédive summoned a new cabinet, giving the leadership to Sherif Pasha, as minister of foreign affairs. What should be done with Arabi was the question of paramount interest, when once the khédive's authority was re-established and recognized. Tewfix and his ministers, if left to themselves, would unquestionably have taken his life ; for in the Orient an unsuccessful revolutionist knows but one fate. But England was determined that Arabi should have a fair trial. To secure this, an irresistible pressure had been brought to bear upon Mr. Gladstone's government by the English press. It was decided that the rebel leaders should appear before a military tribunal, and they were given English counsel to plead their cause. The preliminary negotiations occupied several months, during which time Mr. Broadley and Mr. Napier, Arabi's counsel, became acquainted with the peculiarities of Egyptian legal procedure,[1] and Arabi wrote out his story of the rebellion.[2] The general tenor of his tale was to prove himself innocent of the charge of rebellion. He declared that Tewfik was the traitor ; for the sultan, the real sovereign of Egypt, encouraged the resistance against England that the khédive did not dare show. If Arabi

[1] A. M. Broadley, How We Defended Arabi and His Friends : A Story of Egypt and the Egyptians.
[2] Ahmed Arabi, Instructions to My Counsel, in *The Nineteenth Century* October, 1882.

obeyed his sovereign, how could he be a rebel? He vauntingly wrote:

> But the truth is, I am no "rebel." I led the nation in seeking the liberty of our country, and employed all honorable means to this end, respecting the laws, not thinking of self, as others say, but of the welfare of Egypt. I became commander of the troops appointed to defend the country in a lawful manner, and by the order of the Sultan, the Khédive, the Chamber, and with the sanction of the nation. As regards accusations of massacre and incendiarism, I laugh them to scorn.

Such were the words that Arabi wrote in October, when lying in prison in Cairo. If he had stood by them, he would have had the respect of all who had heard the cry of "Egypt for the Egyptians," and to many he would have posed as a hero and a martyr; but within two months he had acknowledged himself guilty of rebellion, and was cringing at the feet of England and all Englishmen.

The trial was a farce. Everything was "cut and dried" beforehand. It was arranged that Arabi was to plead guilty to rebellion, that he was forthwith to be condemned to death by the court, and that the khédive was immediately to commute the sentence to perpetual exile. In fact, the necessary papers were drawn up and signed before the court met for Arabi's trial on December 3. First, the following charge was read [1]:

---

[1] The documents and articles here given are quoted from Mr. Broadley's How We Defended Arabi, pp. 326, 332, 336, and 341.

Ahmed Arabi Pasha, you are charged before us, on the report of the Commission of Inquiry, with the offence of rebellion against his Highness the Khédive, and thereby committing offences against Article 96[1] of the Ottoman Military and Article 59[2] of the Ottoman Penal Code. Are you guilty or not guilty?

Upon Arabi's saying that his counsel would answer for him, Mr. Broadley read the following:

Of my own free will, and by the advice of my counsel, I plead guilty of the charges now read over to me.

An adjournment of several hours was then taken, as a matter of form, we must believe, for the deliberations were all held in advance. Upon reassembling the clerk of the court read the following sentence :

Whereas Ahmed Arabi Pasha has admitted having committed the crime of rebellion in contravention of Article 96 of the Ottoman Military Code and Article 59 of the Ottoman Penal Code; and whereas, in face of this admission, the court has only to apply the articles already cited, which punish the crime of rebellion by the penalty of death; for these motives the court unanimously con-

[1] Art. 96.—All persons who to the number of eight or more revolt, using their arms, and refuse to disperse, or do not cease the revolt on receiving the orders of a superior authority, may be punished with death.

[2] Art. 59.—Whoever, without an order from the Government, or without a legal motive, shall assume the command of a division, a fortified place, or city, *etc.*, and any commander who, without a legitimate motive, shall persist in keeping his troops under arms after their disbandment has been ordered by the Government, may be punished with death.

demns Ahmed Arabi Pasha to death for the crime of rebellion against his Highness the Khédive by application of the said articles and orders. That the said judgment be submitted for the consideration of his Highness the Khédive.

But the judgment had already been submitted, so that the clerk was able to read the following decree from the khédive at once:

We, Mehemet Tewfik, Khédive of Egypt: Whereas Ahmed Arabi Pasha has been condemned to death by judgment of Court Martial of this day's date, by application of Articles 96 of the Military Code and 59 of the Penal Code, and whereas we desire, for reasons of our own, to exercise in reference to the said Ahmed Arabi Pasha the right of pardon which appertains to us exclusively, we have decreed and do decree as follows: The penalty of death pronounced against Ahmed Arabi is commuted to perpetual exile from Egypt and its dependencies. This pardon will be of no effect, and the said Ahmed Arabi will be liable to the penalty of death, if he enters Egypt or its dependencies. Our Ministers of the Interior, War, and Marine are charged with the execution of this decree.

[Signed]   MEHEMET TEWFIK.

Arabi was glad to escape with his life, if we may judge from his profuse thanks. He thanked Mr. Gladstone, Lord Granville, Lord Dufferin, Sir Edward Malet, Mr. Blunt, Mr. Broadley, Mr. Napier, the English people, the English press, and others to whom he felt specially grateful. It is not reported that the khédive was among the number. On the 26th of December Arabi and his six companions, Mahmûd Sami, Yakûb Sami, Mahmûd Fehmy, Tûlba Osmat, Ali Fehmy, and Abd-el-Al Hilmy, upon whom the same sentence had been passed, left Cairo for the Island of Ceylon, there to spend their life of perpetual exile.

All this while France had been chafing under the prospect of the abolition of the Dual Control. England had proposed in its stead a public debt commission, of which she offered the presidency to France, by way of a sop to appease any anger; but Premier Duclerc rejected the proposal. It therefore became necessary for Lord Granville to define the position of England in Egypt. This he did on January 25, 1883, in an identical note to the Powers. He recited that the Anglo-French control had not been the result of international agreement, but of tripartite understanding between England, France, and Egypt; and that, France having withdrawn from Egypt at the beginning of the war, England had to suppress the rebellion without assistance. She now purposed to keep an army of occupation in Egypt only so long as to secure the permanency of the re-established government. Lord Granville announced, further, that England would favor new regulations to provide for the future neutrality and inviolability of the Suez canal. He was careful to insert in his note that the protection of Egypt would be considered the only justification for the military occupation of the canal. He begged that the Powers would alter the capitulations so that foreigners in Egypt might be taxed, a plan, as we have seen, that is contemplated in every scheme of reform, but never carried out. He also suggested the prolongation of the mixed tribunals for another year.[1]

With regard to international matters in Egypt, Lord Granville announced that certain reforms in the army, in the police, and in political institutions had been undertaken.

Reference has already been made to the appointment of Baker Pasha to supervise the reorganization of the Egyptian army. At the beginning of 1883 he was superseded by Sir Evelyn Wood, who undertook to introduce, so far as practicable, a discipline and treatment similar to those employed in the British army. Relieved from the supervision of the army Baker organized a police force of 4,000 men, which was divided into urban and rural constabulary and officered by Englishmen. The reform in political institutions was the work, largely, of Lord Dufferin. He had been sent from Constantinople to Cairo, early in November, with the special mission of bringing order out of governmental chaos. In

---

[1] Their expiration had been fixed for 1881, but two yearly prolongations had already been added to the original term of five years.

two months he had prepared a scheme of legislative reorganization. This was, however, somewhat altered; so that it was not until May, 1883, that the plan in its improved form was accepted by the decree of the khédive.

The new constitution provided for three classes of assemblies : the " Legislative Council," the " General Assembly," and the " Provincial Councils," of which there were to be fourteen, one for each province. The legislative council was to consist of thirty members, fourteen of whom were to be nominated by the khédive, and sixteen of whom were to be elective. Of the latter, one would represent Cairo, another the towns of Alexandria, Damietta, Rosetta, Suez, Port Said, Ismailia, and El-Azich, and the remaining fourteen would represent each one a province. The elective members were to be chosen for terms of six years, and might be indefinitely re-elected. The council was to meet as often as once in two months. Its influence on legislation was to be so great, says Mr. Amos,[1] that " it is hardly conceivable that a law could be persisted in, in the face of a determined remonstrance of the legislative council." No law or decree of a legislative character could be promulgated unless the government had obtained the opinion of the

[1] Sheldon Amos, The New Egyptian Constitution, in *The Contemporary Review*, June, 1883.

council. If it should dissent from that opinion, the government must give its reasons. A special article provided that the budget must be submitted, and that the council might express its opinion and wishes on each section thereof. The reasons for dissent must be given as in other cases. The legislative council was to have, further, the right to discuss freely the condition of the country and to consider any needful legislative reforms, and to call for the drafting of measures, to be submitted to itself, which should serve as the basis of legislation.

The general assembly was to consist of eighty-four members : the eight ministers of state, the thirty members of the legislative counsel, and forty-six elected members. The latter were to be elected for terms of six years and, like the members of the legislative council, might be indefinitely re-elected. The assembly must meet as often as once in two years, and its functions were to be largely of a financial character. No new tax could be levied unless it should receive the vote of the assembly, and no public loan could be contracted unless the assembly should be consulted. The reasons of dissent on the part of the government must be given to the assembly, as to the legislative council.

The fourteen provincial councils were to consist each one of from four to eight members, and were to divide between them the representation of the six thousand villages in Egypt. Considerable legislative power in local government was to be given them, such as voting of extraordinary taxes for local improvement, which were to take effect merely upon the sanction of the government. Every Egyptian man, over twenty years of age, was to vote (by ballot) for an " elector-delegate " from the village in the neighborhood of which he lived, and the " electors-delegate " from all the villages in a province were to form the constituency that should elect the provincial council. The term and re-eligibility of the members of the provincial council were to be the same as those of members of the other two bodies, except that at the end of three years one-half of the provincial council was to be renewed by lot. The " electors-delegate " were also to elect directly the forty-six elective members of the general assembly ; but they were to have no share in the election of members of the legislative council. Each provincial council was to elect from its own number one member of the legislative council.

Such, in brief, was the scheme that Lord Dufferin proposed and the khédive sanctioned. It was well received by many who thought that it promised a brilliant future for Egypt. The idea, however, of looking to the fellahîn of Egypt for the exercise of constitutional rights and duties strikes any one who is acquainted with their abject condition and disposition as almost absurd. It is well enough for the Westerner to import the ideas that have been the slow growth of centuries in the most highly civilized lands; they will have their influence; and yet it must always be borne in mind that the political idea is the fruit only of internal growth. Lord Dufferin framed the constitution; but he knew that the chiefest truth among his recommendations lay in the following paragraph:

> The chief requirement of Egypt is justice. A pure, cheap, and simple system of justice will prove more beneficial to the country than the largest constitutional privileges. The structure of society in the East is so simple that, provided the taxes are righteously assessed, it does not require much law-making to make the people happy.

The scheme for reorganization was carried forward to the extent of electing the "electors-delegate" in September; but by that time Egypt was again in a state of such disquietude that the British advisers of the khédive considered it unwise to put the new institutions into operation. In place of legislative council and general assembly, the khédive appointed a council of state, consisting of eleven Egyptians, two Armenians, and ten Europeans. The reforms were set aside for the time being in view of impending troubles and dangers in the Sûdan.

VII.

THE SÛDAN AND THE MAHDI.

THE Sûdan comprises the vast region lying between the equator and the southern boundary of Egypt at the first cataract of the Nile, and extending from the Red Sea and Abyssinia on the east to a western indefiniteness—to the point, one might say, from which a slave could be carried to the Nile with some chance of profit to the slave-hunter. Since the day of Mehemet Ali, the country had been to Egypt very much what Egypt was to Turkey before the day of the great pasha. Mehemet Ali appropriated the Sûdan to himself with that freehanded robbery that was characteristic of power in the time of feudalism, and his successors, excepting perhaps Said, did all they could to keep up the system of robbery and spoliation that he had begun. On the other hand, the chiefs of the native tribes did all they could to resist the power of Egypt, often even to the point of bloodshed and murder; or paid their enforced tributes unwillingly and only after these had been diminished by all possible peculations. There was an extensive inland commerce in the Sûdan that made it a valuable province. The yield of ivory, ostrich feathers, grains, and tropical fruits was very large; but the traffic in slaves was the great industry of the country. The Sûdan supplied the slave markets of the Eastern world. It was this feature of commerce that first attracted the attention of the West to the Sûdan. It was the motive of mercy that encouraged the interference of civilized people.

Ismail, with all the ambition of Mehemet Ali, was ready to listen to any plans for increasing his authority, especially if they were suggested by Europeans. He had long entertained a scheme of aggrandizement in the Sûdan; and he fancied that expeditions to suppress the slave-trade, if organized in his name, would somehow secure the extension of his power. It may be doubted if he appreciated the humanitarian motives that suggested to Englishmen the necessity of such an expedition as Sir Samuel W. Baker was deputed to lead in 1869; but he gave Sir Samuel his hearty co-operation, and appointed him governor-general of the entire region south of Gondokoro. Several years before that time Ismail had reasserted Egypt's authority, which had been suffered to lapse through the inactivity of Said and the opposition of the Sûdanese, by an extension of his dominion to the west in the conquest of Darfûr; and now he was glad to have his governor-general push on to the south. The story of Sir Samuel's attempt to reach his province, and of his success in abolishing the slave-traffic only for the time that the slave-posts were under his eye, is told in his own book, *Ismailia*. It is enough to state here that, despite his strenuous and most worthy efforts, he made no permanent impression upon the trade he sought to wipe out; on the contrary, by his opposition to the most influential men of the Sûdan, the slave-traders, he brought Egypt into greater odium then before, and increased the hatred that had always been felt for Egyptian rule.

The successor of Sir Samuel Baker was Colonel Charles George Gordon, familiarly known as "Chinese Gordon" from his remarkable career in the suppression of the Tai-ping rebellion in China. He was, perhaps, the most humane man in England; but his character was as firm as it was sweet, and his courage was as great as his pity. Of the man whose name has been for years a household word among the civilized and the heathen, whose feats have won the admiration of the world, and whose charities have been the inspiration of the rich and the comfort of the poor, further characterization is needless. Suffice it to say that Gordon had the qualities that fitted him pre-eminently for the work he undertook when, in 1874, he started upon his mission to the Sûdan. He did not give Ismail credit for much philanthropy; for, before he left Cairo for Khartûm, he wrote to England:

I think I can see the true motive of the expedition, and believe it to be a sham to catch the attention of the English people: and feel like a Gordon who has been humbugged.[1]

Going to the Equatorial Province, however, solely on the authority of Ismail, he did not question the latter's motives too closely, but applied himself to the work of the expedition. He was to establish a series of posts between Khartum and Gondokoro and to suppress the slave-trade. In eighteen months Gordon returned to Cairo and resigned his commission under the khédive. This is what he had done at that time:

He had mapped the White Nile from Khartûm to within a short distance of the Victoria Nyanza. He had given to the slave-trade on the White Nile a deadly blow. He had restored confidence and peace among the tribes of the Nile valley, so that they now freely brought into the stations their beef, corn, and ivory for sale. He had opened up the water communication between Gondokoro and the Lakes. He had established satisfactory relations with King M'tesa. He had formed Government districts, and established secure posts with safe communication between them. He had contributed a revenue to the Khé-

[1] Archibald Forbes, Chinese Gordon, p. 125.

divial exchequer, and this without oppression. The Taiping Rebellion established Gordon's genius as a military commander; the Equatorial Provinces, when he left them, testified not less to his genius as a philanthropic and practical administrator.[1]

Gordon resigned because Ismail Yakûb, the governor-general of the Sûdan, threw so many stumbling-blocks in his way. While he was doing all he could to suppress the slave-trade, Ismail Yakûb was doing all he could to foster it. At the beginning of 1877 the khédive removed the latter, and wrote the following to Gordon (February 17) :

> Setting a just value on your honorable character, on your zeal, and on the great services you have already done me, I have resolved to bring the Sûdan, Darfûr, and the provinces of the Equator, into one vast province, and place it under you as Governor-General.[2]

Gordon accepted the larger responsibilities and duties of the office bestowed upon him. For two years and more he worked with indomitable energy in crushing the slave-traffic, in putting down insurrection, and in establishing his authority throughout the vast provinces nominally under his control. In spite of almost insuperable difficulties in the way of inadequate resources, both military[3] and financial, he accomplished wonders. If he had been content

[1] Ibid., p. 157.   [2] Ibid., p. 159.
[3] "The Sûdan had been well-nigh drained of troops for the support of the sultan in his war with Russia." Ibid., p. 162.

to remain at Khartûm after the fall of Ismail, the fame and fear of the False Prophet might never have been known in Egypt ; but he was disgusted with the abdication, and insisted upon resigning, to the no small relief, probably, of the new khédive and his ministers, who were glad to be rid of all the servants of Ismail.

After Gordon left the Sûdan, in 1879, an Egyptian pasha was appointed governor-general, and the country relapsed into its former feeling of bitterness toward Egyptian rule. It was not long before the disaffection found its leader. He was no less a person than the Mahdi, whose coming had been foretold by the prophet Mohammed. He chose an opportune moment to act as the champion of his people. They had been incensed at the suppression of the slave-trade, they hated the Egyptian rule, and they believed that the fourteenth century of the Hegira, which was close at hand, would, in accordance with prophecy, usher in an era of unexampled prosperity and happiness.

Mehemet Ahmed, who called himself the Mahdi, was an obscure carpenter's son, who had studied religious creeds with one sect of dervishes in Khartûm and with another sect in Berber until 1870, when he became a *fakir*, or dervish-chief, himself. He then retired to the island of Abba, on the White Nile, where he became famed for his piety. He lived in a cave, and gave himself up to prayers, fastings, and mortifications of the flesh. He won a wide notoriety, and made many disciples. Rich gifts were bestowed upon him, and the neighboring sheikhs gladly gave him their daughters in marriage. His brotherhood in Khartûm heard of his devotion, wealth, and influence, and sent to him, early in 1881, a messenger to bid him arise, in answer to the call of God, and lead a great army. Mehemet Ahmed took up the sword at once, and in May declared to the *fakirs* of the faith of the Shiites that he was the Imam Mahdi, the new Messiah who had come to lead new believers into the fold of Islam, and to annihilate all the infidels on the face of the earth. His declaration met with no denial among the Shiites, whose religious order was confined almost wholly to the Sûdan; but at Cairo, Constantinople, and Mecca, the report of a Mahdi was scoffed at. Where were the signs[1] and portents that should herald his coming?

[1] The greater signs, among which the coming of the Mahdi is reckoned, are seventeen in all, and it must be confessed that some at least among these seem unlikely to be, for the present, literally fulfilled. The sun must rise in the west; the beast must emerge from the earth near Mecca; the walls of Stambûl must fall by miracle before an invading foe; the *Messîh ed-Dejâl*, or 'Lying Anointed One,' marked K F R on his forehead, one-eyed, and riding from Irak on an ass, must lay waste the earth. The true Messiah (our Lord Jesus) must appear on the minaret at Damascus, must reign in Jerusalem, and defeat Gog and Magog, and slay ed-Dejâl at the gate of Lydda. A massacre of the Jews, and invasion of Syria by the great giants (Gog and Magog), who are to drink dry the sea of

But the Mahdi set about the establishment of "a universal equality, a universal law, a universal religion, and a community of goods,"[1] and swore that he would visit with death all who did not believe in and follow him. In August, Raûf Pasha, the governor-general of the Sûdan, became alarmed at the growing power of the False Prophet,—for such he had been declared by the ulemas of Constantinople and Cairo and the Grand Sherif of Mecca, the highest priest of Islam,—and he sent an army to crush him. But the Mahdi easily repulsed the Egyptian[2] force, as he did also a stronger force sent against him at the end of 1881. In June, 1882, he fought his first great battle, and won a brilliant victory. Abdel Kadir, who had succeeded Raûf Pasha as governor-general, sent out the strongest force he could muster; but it was overwelmingly defeated by the Mahdi's fanatical followers. Not a

Galilee, a smoke which shall fill the world, a relapse of Arabia into paganism, the discovery of hid treasures in the Euphrates, the destruction of the Kaaba by negroes, beasts and stones speaking with human voices, a fire of Yemen, a man of the sons of Kahtan, wielding a rod, and an icy wind from Damascus which shall sweep away the souls of all who have faith as a grain of mustard-seed, and blow to heaven the Koran itself; these are the wonders which, together with the coming of the Mahdi, will prepare the way for the tremendous *Yôssr ed Dîn*, or final day of judgment."— C. R. Conder, The Guide of Islam, in *The Fortnightly Review*.

[1] A. Egmont Hake, The Story of Chinese Gordon, vol. ii., p. 24.
[2] The government forces in the Sûdan were in large part made up of Egyptian soldiers, the Sûdanese soldiers being sent to Egypt in at least equal numbers. This exchange of military was held one of the chief grievances against Egyptian rule.

commander escaped with his life, and nearly every Egyptian soldier perished. And now for a time the False Prophet had things pretty much his own way. Arabi's rebellion not only diverted attention from the Sûdan, but it drew largely upon the Sûdanese garrisons for troops to support the nationalist cause. The Mahdi became more and more aggressive, and his ranks and his coffers were continually filling. But, in attacking El Obeid, he was repulsed with heavy loss. He was beaten off only temporarily, however; for he soon returned and laid siege to the garrison, which was finally compelled to yield, January 15, 1883. The commander of the garrison and many of his subordinates saved their lives by taking service under the Mahdi's standard.

The news of the fall of Obeid reached Egypt about the beginning of February. The insurrection was sufficiently serious to demand the attention of the khédive. Lord Dufferin, however, advised letting the Mahdi alone so long as he remained in Kordofan. But the Egyptian government determined upon an expedition, and entrusted its command to Colonel Hicks, a retired English officer. It was impossible, so soon after Arabi's rebellion, to send as strong a force as was desirable. The expedition consisted of eight English officers, 6,000 infantry, 1,000 irregulars, 500 cavalry, and a small force of artillery. The English government in no way sanctioned the undertaking, nor did they oppose it. Lord Granville gave Sir Edward Malet, the British consul at Cairo, positive orders not to offer any advice on the question. After the first engagement between Hicks and the rebels, April 9, in which the former achieved a brilliant success, Hicks made many appeals to Malet for reinforcements; but the latter merely passed them on to the Egyptian government without comment. As Mr. McCarthy puts it,

Though England had interfered in Egypt by force of arms to keep the khédive on his throne, though Cairo was occupied by English soldiers, though it was clearly in England's power, and in her right, to counsel the Egyptian ministry as to the course they should pursue in the most difficult of all Egyptian questions, the ministry still affected to keep up the absurd pretense of exercising no influence upon the councils of Egypt.[1]

England could not shirk her responsibility by keeping silent. She was bound in all honor to give her advice at least; and refusing, she failed of her just duty and obligations.[2]

The summer and the rainy season of 1883 were passed by Hicks Pasha in Khartûm; but on the

[1] Justin McCarthy, England Under Gladstone, ch. xv.
[2] "Why, then, it may be asked, did not the Liberal Government use its influence to prohibit General Hicks's useless expedition? The question very plausibly suggests English responsibility for the expedition, and the consequences, or supposed consequences of its failure." English Policy in the Sûdan, *British Quarterly Review*, July, 1884.

9th of September he set out for El Obeid, the stronghold of the Mahdi. The story of his march and the details of the final tragedy will probably never be authentically told. The last bits of news were in the letters of Edmund O'Donovan to a London newspaper. He seems to have appreciated the dangers of the expedition. On September 23, he wrote to a friend :

It would be odd if the next intelligence from this part of the world told that I, too, had gone the way of all flesh. However, to die even out here, with a lance-head as big as a shovel through me, will meet my views better than the slow, gradual sinking into the grave which is the lot of so many. . . . You know I am by this time, after an experience of many years, pretty well accustomed to dangers of most kinds, even some *extra*. Yet I assure you I feel it terrible to face deadly peril far away from civilized ideas, and where no mercy is to be met with, in company with cravens that you expect to see run at every moment, and who will leave you behind to face the worst.

When this friend next heard of O'Donovan, he had " gone the way of all flesh."

The accepted account of the slaughter of Hicks Pasha's army of 11,000 men is that, having been treacherously led into an ambuscade on the 1st or 2d of November, they fought for three days with the courage and hopelessness of that smaller band under Leonidas at Thermopylæ ; then, overcome with heat, thirst, and fatigue, their ammunition gone, they fell where they had fought, before the fury of the Mahdi's hordes. All the Egyptians were massacred, and only one European is known to have escaped.

It was more than two weeks before the terrible news reached Khartûm and was telegraphed to Cairo. It would be difficult to say whether the panic was greater in Egypt or in the Sûdan. In the Sûdan, governors of provinces, at the report of the Mahdi's victory, declared their allegiance to the holy cause, and flocked to his capital with troops and treasure. Nothing succeeds like success. The vast region from Kordofan to the equator was kindled to a fanatical zeal. The route from Khartnm to Sûakim, on the Red Sea, was intercepted by a lieutenant of the Mahdi's. The grasp of the Mahdi seemed to be closing about Khartûm. Colonel de Coetlogen, with his slender garrison of 4,000, could not hold that city before the sweep of the rebel forces. In Cairo the consternation was no greater over the defeat than over England's opposition to an expedition to crush the Mahdi. Lord Granville telegraphed to Sir Evelyn Baring, who was now the British representative in Egypt, that the government would lend neither English nor Indian troops to assist an expedition. He advised the abandonment of the Sûdan. But the khédive's ministers said that they could not give up the territory that belonged to the sultan, and of which Egypt was simply the guardian. While negotiations between England and Egypt were pending, the khédive's government decided to send a force to Sûakim to relieve the beleaguered Egyptian garrisons at Sinkat and Tokar, and open the route from the Red Sea to Berber, so as to allow the Egyptians in Khartûm a way of escape. The expedition was placed under the command of Baker Pasha.

But now, January 4, 1884, Mr. Gladstone's government expressed its advice more forcibly than a month before.

It is indispensable [wrote Lord Granville] that her Majesty's Government should, as long as the provisional occupation of the country by English troops continues, be assured that the advice which, after full consideration of the Egyptian Government, they may feel it their duty to tender to the Khédive should be followed. It should be made clear to the Egyptian ministers and governors of the provinces that the responsibility which, for the time, rests on England, obliges her Majesty's Government to insist on the adoption of the policy which they recommend; and that it will be necessary that those ministers and governors who do not follow this course should cease to hold their offices.

This was what Mr. McCarthy calls "interference with a vengeance."[1] It was the decisive, if tardy,

[1] England Under Gladstone, ch. xv.

assertion of authority. The note was equivalent to saying that, in future, England's will was to be the law of Egypt. From Downing Street the order was issued that the Sûdan must be abandoned, whereupon Sherif's ministry resigned. Nubar Pasha was called to his place; and he telegraphed at once, of course at England's dictation, to Baker, at Sûakim, that he must prepare for evacuation.

But the question now presented itself: How should the evacuation be effected? The answer was furnished by the *Pall Mall Gazette*, of London. Its issue of January 9 contained the following suggestion:

At present it is obviously out of the question to send an army of relief to Colonel Coetlogen. Baker Pasha's force seems inadequate even to relieve Sinkat. In common with the ex-Khédive, of whom he speaks with remarkable cordiality, General Gordon deprecates the despatch of either Indian or English troops to the Sûdan. But if we have not an Egyptian army to employ in the service, and if we must not send an English force, what are we to do? There is only one thing that we can do. We cannot send a regiment to Khartûm, but we can send a man who, on more than one occasion, has proved himself more valuable in similar circumstances than an entire army. Why not send Chinese Gordon with full powers to Khartûm, to assume absolute control of the territory, to treat with the Mahdi, to relieve the garrisons, and do what can be done to save what can be saved from the wreck in the Sûdan? . . . No one can deny the urgent need in the midst of that hideous welter of confusion for the presence of such a man, with a born genius for command, an unexampled capacity in organizing "ever-victorious armies," and a perfect knowledge of the Sûdan and its people. Why not send him out with *carte blanche* to do the best that can be done? He may not be able single-handed to reduce that raging chaos to order, but the attempt is worth making, and if it is to be made, it will have to be made at once.

The popular feeling was found to be heartily in accord with this suggestion, and a clamor was immediately raised on all sides for the dispatch of Gordon to the Sûdan. The British government, some weeks before, had offered to appoint an English officer to go to Khartûm and organize the evacuation; but the Egyptian ministry had not taken up the offer. Now, however, Nubar informed Sir Evelyn Baring that such an appointment would be accepted. The British government, therefore, at once communicated with Gordon, recalling him from Brussels on the 17th of January where he had just arrived to receive the last instructions of the king of Belgium, before proceeding on an antislavery mission to the Congo. He returned to London that same day, and on the morning of the 18th was closeted with members of the English cabinet. On Saturday, the 19th the London *Times* startled the world with the following announcement:

It will be a welcome surprise to the country to learn that General Gordon started last night, not for the Congo, but for Egypt. . . . He takes with him, as his military secretary, Lieutenant-Colonel Stewart, who was on duty at Khartûm so late as last year, and whose knowledge of the affairs of the Sûdan is second only to that of General Gordon himself. The immediate purpose of the General's mission is, we understand, to report on the military situation in the Sûdan, to provide in the best manner for the safety of the European population of Khartûm and of the Egyptian garrisons still in the country, as well as for the evacuation of the Sûdan with the exception of the seaboard. His appointment will be received by the country with a certain sense of relief, as showing that the Government has been willing to seek the best advice and to select the most competent agent for the development of its policy in the Sûdan.

VIII.

THE MISSION OF GORDON.—OPERATIONS IN THE EASTERN SÛDAN.

ENGLAND had now taken a firm stand. She largely increased her responsibilities by entrusting Gordon with the Sûdanese mission. She had been niggardly even with advice in the case of Hicks, but she was ready to hazard all with Gordon. Her unquestionable responsibility will be proved by the following documents. The day that Gordon left London, Lord Granville gave him this note of instruction :

FOREIGN OFFICE, Jan. 18th, 1884.

Sir :—Her Majesty's Government are desirous that you should proceed at once to Egypt, to report to them on the military situation in the Sûdan and on the measures which it may be advisable to take for the security of the Egyptian garrisons still holding possession in that country, and for the safety of the European population in Khartûm. You are also desired to consider and report upon the best mode of effecting the evacuation of the interior of the Sûdan, and upon the manner in which the safety and the good administration by the Egyptian

Government of the ports on the seacoast can best be secured. In connection with this subject, you should pay especial consideration to the question of the steps that may usefully be taken to counteract the stimulus which it is feared may possibly be given to the slave trade by the present insurrectionary movement and by the withdrawal of the Egyptian authority from the interior. You will be under the instructions of her Majesty's agent and Consul-General at Cairo, through whom your reports to her Majesty's Government should be sent under flying seal. You will consider yourself authorized and instructed to perform such other duties as the Egyptian Government may desire to entrust to you, and as may be communicated to you by Sir E. Baring. You will be accompanied by Colonel Stewart, who will assist you in the duties thus confided to you. On your arrival in Egypt you will at once communicate with Sir E. Baring, who will arrange to meet you, and will settle with you whether you should proceed direct to Sûakim, or should go yourself or despatch Colonel Stewart to Khartûm, *via* the Nile.

I am, *etc.*,   GRANVILLE.

While Gordon was on his way to Egypt he wrote the following notes, explanatory of the above instructions, and developed in accordance with the views expressed at the conference on January 18. These notes were forwarded from Cairo to the Foreign Office at London.

1. I understand that her Majesty's Government have come to the irrevocable decision not to incur the very

onerous duty of securing to the peoples of the Sûdan a just future government. That, as a consequence, her Majesty's Government have determined to restore to these peoples their independence, and will no longer suffer the Egyptian Government to interfere with their affairs.

2. For this purpose her Majesty's Government have decided to send me to the Sûdan to arrange for the evacuation of these countries, and the safe removal of the Egyptian employés and troops.

3. Keeping paragraph 1 in view, *viz.*, that the evacuation of the Sûdan is irrevocably decided on, it will depend on circumstances in what way this is to be accomplished. My idea is that the restoration of the country should be made to the different petty Sultans who existed at the time of Mehemet Ali's conquest, and whose families still exist; that the Mahdi should be left altogether out of the calculation as regards the handing over the country; and that it should be optional with the Sultans to accept his supremacy or not. As these Sultans would probably not be likely to gain by accepting the Mahdi as their sovereign, it is probable that they will hold to their independent positions. Thus we should have two factors to deal with; namely, the petty Sultans asserting their several independence, and the Mahdi's party aiming at supremacy over them. To hand, therefore, over to the Mahdi the arsenals, *etc.*, would, I consider, be a mistake. They should be handed over to the Sultans of the states in which they are placed. The most difficult question is how and to whom to hand over the arsenals of Khartûm, Dongola, and Kassala, which towns have, so to say, no old standing families, Khartûm and Kassala having sprung

up since Mehemet Ali's conquest. Probably it would be advisable to postpone any decision as to these towns till such time as the inhabitants have made known their opinion.

4. I have, in paragraph 3, postponed the transfer of the lands to the local Sultans, and stated my opinion that these will not accept the supremacy of the Mahdi. If this is agreed to and my supposition is correct as to their action, there can be but little doubt that, as far as he is able, the Mahdi will endeavor to assert his rule over them, and will be opposed to any evacuation of the Government employés and troops. My opinion of the Mahdi's force is, that the bulk of those who were with him at Obeid will refuse to cross the Nile, and that those who do so will not exceed 3000 or 4000 men; and also, that these will be composed principally of black troops who have deserted, and who, if offered fair terms, would come over to the Government side. In such a case, *viz.*, " Sultans accepting transfer of territory and refusing the supremacy of the Mahdi, and Mahdi's troops coming over to the Government," resulting weakness of the Mahdi, what should be done should the Mahdi's adherents attack the evacuating columns? It cannot be supposed that these are to offer no resistance, and if in resisting they should obtain a success, it would be but reasonable to allow them to follow up the Mahdi to such a position as would insure their future safe march. This is one of those difficult questions which our Government can hardly be expected to answer, but which may arise, and to which I would call attention. Paragraph 1 fixes irrevocably the decision of the Government, *viz.*, to evacuate the territory, and, of course, as far as possible, involves the avoidance

of any fighting. I can therefore only say, that having in view paragraph 1, and seeing the difficulty of asking her Majesty's Government to give a decision or direction as to what should be done in certain cases, that I will carry out the evacuation as far as possible according to their wish to the best of my ability, and with avoidance, as far as possible, of all fighting. I would, however, hope that her Majesty's Government will give me their support and consideration, should I be unable to fulfill all their expectations.

5. Though it is out of my province to give any opinion as to the action of her Majesty's Government in leaving the Sûdan, still, I must say it would be an iniquity to reconquer these peoples, and then hand them back to the Egyptians without guaranties of future good government. It is evident that this we cannot secure without an inordinate expenditure of men and money. The Sûdan is a useless possession, ever was so, and ever will be so. Larger than Germany, France, and Spain together, and mostly barren, it cannot be governed except by a Dictator, who may be good or bad. If bad, he will cause constant revolts. No one who has ever lived in the Sûdan can escape the reflection: "What a useless possession is this land." Few men can stand its fearful monotony and deadly climate.

6. Said Pasha, the Viceroy before Ismail, went up to the Sûdan with Count F. de Lesseps. He was so discouraged and horrified at the misery of the people, that at Berber Count de Lesseps saw him throw his gun into the river, declaring that he would be no party to such oppression. It was only after the urgent solicitation of European consuls that he reconsidered his decision.

Therefore, I think her Majesty's Government are fully justified in recommending the evacuation, inasmuch as the sacrifice necessary toward securing a good government would be far too onerous to admit of such an attempt being made. Indeed, one may say it is impracticable at any cost. Her Majesty's Government will now leave them as God has placed them; they are not forced to fight among themselves, and they will no longer be oppressed by men coming from lands so remote as Circassia, Kurdistan, and Anatolia.

Colonel Stewart, also, while on the way to Cairo, addressed some observations to the Foreign Office, of which the following is of some importance as showing Gordon's independence of Egypt and direct dependence upon England as the authority of his actions :

I, of course, understand that General Gordon is going to the Sûdan with full powers to make all arrangements as to its evacuation, and that he is in no way to be interfered with by the Cairo Ministers; also, that any suggestions or remarks that the Cairo Government would wish to make are to be made directly to him and her Majesty's Minister Plenipotentiary, and that no intrigues are to be permitted against his authority. Any other course would, I am persuaded, make his mission a failure.

While Gordon was in Cairo, Sir Evelyn Baring communicated to him the following additional instructions :

Lord Granville "authorized and instructed you to perform such duties as the Egyptian Government may desire to entrust to you, and as may be communicated to you by Sir E. Baring." I have now to indicate to you the views of the Egyptian Government on two of the points to which your special attention was directed by Lord Granville. These are, (1) the measures which it may be advisable to take for the security of the Egyptian garrisons still holding positions in the Sûdan, and for the safety of the European population in Khartûm; (2) the best mode of effecting the evacuation of the interior of the Sûdan. These two points are intimately connected, and may conveniently be considered together. It is believed that the number of Europeans at Khartûm is very small, but it has been estimated by the local authorities that some 10,000 to 15,000 people will wish to move northward from Khartûm only when the Egyptian garrison is withdrawn. These people are native Christians, Egyptian employés, their wives and children, *etc.* The Government of his Highness the Khédive is earnestly solicitous that no effort should be spared to insure the retreat both of these people and of the Egyptian garrison without loss of life. As regards the most opportune time and the best method for effecting the retreat, whether of the garrison or of the civil populations, it is neither necessary nor desirable that you should receive detailed instructions. A short time ago the local authorities pressed strongly on the Egyptian Government the necessity for giving orders for an immediate retreat. Orders were accordingly given to commence at once the withdrawal of the civil population. No sooner, however, had these orders been issued than a telegram was received from the Sûdan, strongly urging that the orders for commencing the retreat should be delayed. Under these circumstances, and in view of the fact that the position at Khartûm is now represented as being less critical for the moment than it was a short time ago, it was thought desirable to modify the orders for the immediate retreat of the civil population, and to await your arrival. You will bear in mind that the main end to be pursued is the evacuation of the Sûdan. This policy was adopted, after a very full discussion, by the Egyptian Government, on the advice of her Majesty's Government. It meets with the full approval of his Highness the Khédive, and of the present Egyptian Ministry. I understand, also, that you entirely concur in the desirability of adopting this policy, and that you think it should on no account be changed. You consider that it may take a few months to carry it out with safety. You are further of opinion that "the restoration of the country should be made to the different petty Sultans who existed at the time of Mehemet Ali's conquest, and whose families still exist"; and that an endeavor should be made to form a confederation of those Sultans. In this view the Egyptian Government entirely concurs. It will, of course, be fully understood that the Egyptian troops are not to be kept in the Sûdan merely with the view to consolidating the power of the new rulers of the country. But the Egyptian Government has the fullest confidence in your judgment, your knowledge of the country, and of your comprehension of the general line of policy to be pursued. You are, therefore, given full discretionary power to retain the troops for such reasonable period as you may think necessary, in order that the abandonment of the country may be accomplished with the least possible risk of life and property. A credit of £100,000 has been opened for you at the Finance Department, and further funds will be supplied to you on your requisition when this sum is exhausted. In undertaking the difficult task which now lies before you, you may feel assured that no effort will be wanting on the part of the Cairo authorities, whether English or Egyptians, to afford you all the co-operation and support in their power.

On the 26th of January, General Gordon, Colonel Stewart, and the newly-appointed sultan of Darfur,[1] with no escort beyond their personal attendants, left Cairo for Khartûm, by way of Siût, Assûan, Wady Halfa, Abû Hamed, and Berber.

While this daring party was hastening toward Khartûm as swiftly as railway, steamer, and camel could carry them, events of a portentous nature were occurring elsewhere. On the 5th of February the British Parliament was opened, and on the same day the news was received in London that Baker Pasha had been defeated near Tokar, with a loss of 2,000 men, and had fallen back with the remainder of his army—some 1,200—on Trinkitat, himself escaping death by a reckless dash through the Arab ranks. Osman Digna, the Mahdi's lieutenant, had carried all before him. Trinkitat could not hold out against him, and fears were entertained even for Sûakim, although Admiral Hewett had just landed a force there. These were not favorable

[1] The khédivè had reinstated the heir to the sultanship, who was a captive in Cairo, as the first step toward carrying out Gordon's policy.

auspices for the opening of Parliament. The customary placid language of the Queen's speech was strangely at variance with the feelings of those who listened to it. A vote of censure upon the government was at once moved, but it was rejected in the form offered, and the subject was postponed for a few days. In the meantime public opinion on the necessity of active interference and responsibility had strengthened to the point of insistance. The London *Times* voiced the widespread sentiment in saying :

> This fatuous effort to evade the grasp of facts must now be abandoned, and even with respect to the past the world will be obstinately incredulous. Not only in Europe, as may be seen from the strong language used by the French press, but among the Mohammedan populations of the East, England is held to be responsible for the expeditions of Hicks Pasha and Baker Pasha not less than for the mission of General Gordon.[1]

The excitement caused by the news of Baker's defeat was further increased by the report of the slaughter of the Sinkat garrison. Baker's expedition had utterly failed in the offensive. The vote of censure came on the 12th. The identical motion was offered in the upper House by Lord Salisbury, and in the lower House by Sir Stafford Northcote :

That this House, having read and considered the cor-

---

[1] *The Times*, Feb. 7, 1884.

respondence relating to Egypt, laid on the table by her Majesty's command, is of opinion that the recent lamentable events in the Sûdan are due, in a great measure, to the vacillating and inconsistent policy pursued by her Majesty's Government.

The motion was carried against the government by one hundred majority in the House of Lords, but it was lost in the House of Commons, where Mr. Gladstone made an ingenious defence of his policy of non-intervention, and of his claim of irresponsibility for the slaughter of the Hicks and the defeat of the Baker expedition. Relief had not been sent to Sinkat, because it was believed that such a move would ·endanger the lives of Gordon and those whom he had been sent to rescue, and the chief desire of her Majesty's government was to secure the evacuation, the peaceful evacuation, of the interior of the Sûdan. England was the guardian of Egyptian interests, and the welfare of the land demanded that Gordon's mission should be successfully executed. " For," said Mr. Gladstone, " I look upon the possession of the Sûdan—I won't say as a crime—that would be going a great deal too far—but I look upon it as the calamity of Egypt. It has been a drain on her treasury, it has been a drain on her men." The government was saved in the Commons by a majority of forty-nine.

In spite, now, of the reasons assigned for not

having rescued the garrison of Sinkat, the English government authorized the dispatch of General Graham for the relief of Tokar, Admiral Hewett having already, with English sanction, assumed the general command of forces at Sûakim. Before Graham had landed his force at Trinkitat, however, Tokar had succumbed, the greater part of the garrison joining the standard of Osman Digna. On the last day of February, Graham marched forth and met and overcame the intrepid lieutenant of the Mahdi on the field where Baker's force had been defeated. This success was followed up by further advances, and on March 13 a decisive victory was won. The backbone of the Mahdi's power in the eastern Sûdan seemed broken. But at this juncture General Graham was ordered to embark his troops and leave the seat of war at once. This was a fatal order. Then was the time, Osman's forces having been beaten and scattered, to open the route from Sûakim to Berber, and afford an egress for the garrisons of the interior. The opportunity was missed and never was presented again. Osman gathered together his forces, strengthened his power at his leisure, and held himself in readiness to carry out his old threat of sweeping Sûakim and every soul it contained into the Red Sea.

IX.

GORDON AT KHARTUM, AND THE GOVERNMENT IN LONDON.

WE left General Gordon on his way to Khartûm. He arrived there on February 18. At Berber he had issued a proclamation declaring the purpose and policy of his mission. He had come to establish tranquillity and prevent the shedding of Moslem blood ; to secure to the inhabitants their rights of property, and to put an end to injustice and oppression. He reduced the taxes one-half, and wiped off all arrearages. He conferred upon the people the right, of which they had been deprived at the expense of time, treasure, and blood, to hold slaves as property, with full control over their services. He guaranteed them the privileges they enjoyed under Said Pasha, and promised prosperity and happiness. In consequence of this proclamation Gordon's journey from Berber to Khartûm was a triumphal march. The natives flocked to bless him as their king and deliverer, and he was received at Khartûm with cries of rejoicing.

His proclamation had a very different effect in the outside world. European nations stood aghast. Gordon, the arch enemy of the slave-trade, declared himself its friend! England received the news with consternation and horror. Every Wilberforce of the nation raised his voice of protest. The clamor precipitated a second vote of censure, which was offered by M. Labouchere on March 15, the ground of censure, however, being nominally the useless waste of life in the operations about Sûakim. The government barely escaped defeat, the majority being only seventeen. The criticism on General Gordon for his slave-trade proclamation was as blind as his policy was far-sighted. He had been sent to secure the evacuation of the Sûdan, after which every sane man knew the country would return to its old traffic; for Gordon could scarcely be expected to say: We are to withdraw, but you are to frown upon the slave-trade just as though we were here to compel you. The peaceful evacuation, Gordon well knew, could only be secured by conciliation, and the best favors to grant were those the people were bound to gain. The wisdom of his proclamation needed no further proof than the excessive friendliness of the greetings along his march and of his reception at Khartûm.

Gordon devoted his first day in Khartûm to acts of mercy. He said to the people: "I come without soldiers, but with God on my side, to redress the evils of this land. I will not fight with any weapons but justice." He won the hearts of all at once by burning the government books and all instruments of torment and torture, by releasing the unjustly imprisoned, and by devoting himself personally to the sick and the wronged. That first day, also, he sent a dispatch to Sir Evelyn Baring, saying that it would be folly to leave the Sûdan unless some one were to take his place as governor-general. Anarchy and misery would surely ensue. He named Zubair Pasha[1] as the one above all others to select for the position. "He alone," he wrote, " has the ability to rule the Sûdan, and would be universally accepted by the Sûdan." Sir Evelyn Baring forwarded the suggestion the next day to Earl Granville, and heartily urged its adoption, believing, as he said, that Zubair was the only possible man.

It had been supposed, and, in fact, General Gordon himself had so understood it, that he was to have the dictatorial power in the Sûdan that the crisis demanded. The English government, however, immediately repelled the notion of appointing

[1] Zubair had had great power in the Sûdan, where he was king of the slave-traders. He was, at this time, confined in Cairo, his captivity being lightened by a liberal allowance. Zubair was supposed to bear an undying grudge against Gordon, because Gordon had killed his (Zubair's) son in the Sûdan during a previous campaign.

old slave-trading Zubair governor-general. A long series of telegrams passed between Gordon, Baring, and Granville on the subject. Gordon besought and Baring expostulated; but the government was blind to all reason—to everything but the fear of a renewal of the slave-trade, which, in point of fact, was assured the day the evacuation of the Sûdan was decided upon. General Gordon afterward reduced the government's reasoning on this point to a simple form :[1] " I will not send up A., because he will do this ; but I will leave the country to B., who will do exactly the same." Baring telegraphed to Granville (March 9) :

> As regards slavery, it may certainly receive a stimulus from the abandonment of the Sûdan by Egypt; but the despatch of Zubair Pasha to Khartûm will not affect the question one way or the other. No middle course is possible so far as the Sûdan is concerned. We must either virtually annex the country, which is out of the question, or else we must accept the inevitable consequences of abandoment.

But the British government wished to abandon the Sûdan, and yet avoid the "inevitable consequences." Gordon maintained that to prevent anarchy it was necessary to "smash up" the Mahdi, and that Zubair was the only one who had enough influence and prestige of family to do it. Gordon

---

[1] General Gordon's Journal, p. 42. (September 17.)

could not bear the thought of leaving the Sûdan to ruin. He sent, March 8, a further argument, that should have had some weight with the government: " If you do not send Zubair, you have no chance of getting the garrisons away; this is a heavy argument in favor of sending him."

But it was of no use. On March 28, Earl Granville sent a long note to Sir Evelyn Baring, in which he reviewed the discussion at length, and even rehearsed the slavery antecedents of Zubair. It is impossible, after all the months that have intervened since that note was written, to read it dispassionately. Granville wrote :

Her Majesty's Government, on the perusal of General Gordon's advice, were under the impression that he gave undue weight to the assumed necessity of an immediate evacuation of Khartûm, and they inquired whether it was urgent to make an arrangement at once to provide for his successor, expressing a hope that General Gordon would remain for some time.

In other words, her Majesty's government thought that the "necessity of an immediate evacuation" could be more judiciously determined in Downing Street than in Khartûm. The question could be decided certainly more safely. It is not necessary to go through Lord Granville's note in detail. The vain desire is clearly manifest throughout, that Gordon should not *abandon* the Sûdan in *evacuating*.

Gordon said that he could pursue but one course; Granville denied him that, but suggested no alternative. "Let Gordon stay a while : the government will deliberate. So far as is known, he is not in any immediate danger at Khartûm. We will not let Zubair leave Cairo." That was the gist of the note. A week later, Mr Gladstone naïvely remarked that General Gordon could leave Khartûm "at any time if he felt so disposed." Little did he know the fibre of the man's honor if he thought he could, under any conditions, " feel disposed " to desert the garrisons he had been sent to rescue. He felt that the lives of some 29,000 persons, composing the garrisons at Bahr Ghazelle, Sennar, Kassala, Khartûm, Shendy, Berber, Abû Hamed, and Dongola were in his hands. He would not be false to his trust.

The story of Gordon's government at Khartûm, of his dealings with the people, of his sorties against the threatening forces of the Mahdi, and of his untiring zeal and dauntless personal courage, is told in his own journals[1] and dispatches to Sir Evelyn Baring, and in the letters of Mr. Power, the correspondent of the London *Times.* Our concern is less with those details than with the relations exist-

[1] A large and very valuable part of Gordon's journals was lost when Colonel Stewart's party was massacred, in September, 1884. Gordon had entrusted them to that officer, believing that they would be safer than if kept by himself, in Khartûm. Stewart's journals, which Gordon considered very valuable, were lost at the same time. *Vide seq.*

ing between Gordon and the British government. The Egyptian government quite drops out of notice, all negotiations proceeding independently of the Khédive.

From first to last, so long as communication was kept up with Gordon, the British government pursued a policy of opposition to his proposals. His long-continued and persistent calls for Zubair were disregarded. He desired permission to proceed to El Obeid for a peaceful negotiation with the Mahdi, whom he appointed sultan[1] of Kordofan; but he was told to remain at Khartûm. He said that Berber should be relieved, and that the route from Sûakim to Berber should be kept open; instead of this, the British troops were withdrawn from the Red Sea littoral. He desired that Turkish troops should be sent there; but this proposal was vetoed, presumably on diplomatic grounds. He wished to go from Khartûm to Bahr Ghazelle and the Equatorial Provinces; but he was told again not to proceed beyond Khartum. He begged that troops be sent to Wady Halfa and Assûan; but the request was refused. Later he urged the necessity of a British diversion at Berber; but his plea was not heeded. Was it not strange that the English government should have sent Gordon to the Sûdan

[1] The appointment was scornfully rejected by the Mahdi, who sent dervishes to Gordon, ordering him to embrace the Moslem faith.

with the explicit understanding that his judgment should determine the means and methods of evacuation, and then never, in any essential particular, follow his advice? The world called it almost a crime. Early in April, Gordon sent an undated message to Sir Evelyn Baring, containing the following words:

As far as I can understand, the situation is this: You state your intention of not sending any relief up here or to Berber, and you refuse me Zubair. I consider myself free to act according to circumstances. I shall hold on here as long as I can; and if I can suppress the rebellion, I shall do so. If I cannot, I shall retire to the Equator; and leave you the indelible disgrace of abandoning the garrisons of Sennar, Kassala, Berber, and Dongola, with the certainty that you will, eventually, be forced to smash up the Mahdi under great difficulties, if you would retain peace in Egypt.

As Mr. Hake says: "The breach was complete The great soldier declined to serve as an instrument of dishonor."[1]

In England the bitterest criticism was heaped on Mr. Gladstone. The liberals in Parliament became hostile to their own government. On the 12th of May a third vote of censure was proposed, in which the government was charged with indifference to the success of Gordon's mission and the

[1] The Story of Chinese Gordon, vol. ii., p. 166.

safety of his person. Again the government escaped, but with the small majority of 28 in 578 votes cast. The result would probably have been fatal to Mr. Gladstone, if the vote had been postponed for a month. Then his government would have been held responsible for the fall of Berber and the terrible massacre that occurred there on June 2. A fourth vote might have been proposed, had not a different phase of the Egyptian trouble been forced upon Parliament for consideration before the news was received.

As always, the finances of Egypt were in a bad way. For three years the deficits of the treasury had been accumulating, till they amounted to something over £8,000,000. The indemnities for losses sustained in the bombardment, burning, and pillage of Alexandria made about half of this sum ; and the expenditures for the military constituted the chief item in the remaining half. The British government desired to meet the deficit by a new loan ; but as this could not be done without conflicting with the law of liquidation, it was decided to summon to a conference those Powers that had agreed to the establishment of the law. Accordingly, on the 19th of April, Lord Granville sent an identical note to the great Powers, inviting them to a conference in London, to consider whether a modification of the laws of liquidation would not be for the financial interest of Egypt. Germany, Austria, Russia, and Italy accepted the invitation at once; but France, with something of her old-time jealousy, objected to a conference that could not consider the political as well as the financial question. Lord Granville, however, was firm in his insistance upon the limitation, so far as the conference was concerned; but he entered into a diplomatic correspondence with M. Waddington. The result of the exchange of views, or, as it was called, "the Anglo-French agreement," was submitted to Parliament by Mr. Gladstone before the conference met. France resigned all claim of control in Egypt, and agreed never to land troops in the Delta without the consent of England. On the other hand, England agreed to withdraw her military forces from Egypt before the first day of January, 1888, unless the Powers should request the contrary. In the meantime she was to prepare a scheme for the neutralization of Egypt, which should be submitted to the Powers. The *Caisse de la Dette Publique*, it was agreed, should be placed under the multiple direction of the Powers. But all these arrangements, as Mr. Gladstone said, were dependent upon the will of the conference, which, in turn, should be binding upon England, according as Parliament, by its votes, determined.

England being thus carefully guarded behind two

big *ifs*, the Conference met in London on June 28. Its progress was slow, and as it failed of its purpose ultimately, its details need not be given. The Powers so hopelessly disagreed that the Conference was dissolved on the 2d of August. France, the leader of the opposition to England, could not secure the formulation of a future policy. As a last straw she endeavored to obtain an adjournment of the Conference till October, but, instead, it was adjourned *sine die;* and thus, all participation in the affairs of Egypt was lost to her. This was practically accomplished by her withdrawal from a joint supervision at the time of Arabi's rebellion; but now, for the first time, her position of looker-on was determined. Germany seemed satisfied with having egged on France to a point where the refusal of her demands would only increase the growing coolness between the British and French governments. Turkey, of course, had found no following in urging her rights and ability to control Egypt without the help of Eastern Powers. Italy, the only pronounced ally of England in the Conference, retired with the distinction that this alliance had brought upon her, and accepted, as her share of the "spoils," the thanks which Sir John Saville Lumley, British Minister to Italy, was instructed to bestow upon her for the support which she gave to the British proposals in the Conference.

The glory of the collapse of the Conference, if there were any, fell to England. It was demonstrated that the Powers could not control Egypt in unison; it was left to England to do the work alone and to earn the praise or the blame. The financial question remaining still unsettled, the government commissioned Lord Northbrook to go to Egypt and investigate the "condition of affairs so as to advise the English government as to what counsel should be given to the Egyptian government in the present circumstances." Of course it was understood that the "counsel" would be of a more peremptory character than advice usually is; for counsel and command to the khédive have long been regarded in England as one and the same thing. The High Commission found the finances of Egypt in such a muddle that one of two courses seemed inevitable: to make a declaration of bankruptcy with a reduction of the coupons, or to turn the revenues temporarily from the sinking fund for the redemption of the certified debt into the Egyptian treasury. The latter alternative was chosen, and wisely, as it seems, although it was a breach of the law of liquidation. Lord Northbrook held that, if the tribute to Turkey and the expenses of the government could be met for a time, and if the revenues should afterward revert to the sinking fund, the coupon-holders would lose less than by a declaration of bankruptcy. By a decree of the khédive, September 18, the law of liquidation was suspended for six weeks. This called forth the united remonstrance of the Powers. The plan, however, was persisted in.

General Gordon, meanwhile, seemed to have dropped completely out of mind. No word had been received from him since May. By the fall of Berber telegraphic communications had been cut off, and only the vaguest rumors from any point south of Dongola made their way to Cairo. At the eleventh hour there had been a pretence of opening the route from Sûakim to Berber by sending a railway plant to Sûakim. Desultory dispatches of the progress in its construction and of skirmishes with Osman Digna were received during the summer; but no one was surprised that the work was discontinued before autumn. This railway scheme was perhaps less of a farce than the Khédive Ismail's projected railway from Wady Halfa south to Hanneck; for Ismail left his plant to be covered by the sweeping sands of the Nubian desert, while the English carried theirs off to India. In order to divert attention from the Berber massacre, the success of Admiral Hewett's mission to King John of Abyssinia, the news of which had been received at about the same time, was somewhat magnified. He secured, by treaty, access to a third route to Khartûm from Massowah through Abyssinia. The sequel has shown how valueless the concession was. But the attention of England had been very generally diverted from Egypt altogether. The Franchise Bill at home had been the absorbing topic during the early summer. There had, however, been many rumors afloat of an expedition to be sent to the relief of General Gordon. But the weeks had drifted by, and July, the month first named for the dispatch of the expedition, was past before any active preparations were made. These were begun in August by the vote of a credit of £300,000 to defray expenses. It seemed, finally, as if the conscience of the government were quickened.

X.

WOLSELEY'S EXPEDITION.—CONCLUSION.

THE command of the relief expedition was entrusted to Lord Wolseley, the Sir Garnet Wolseley who had suppressed Arabi's rebellion, and thereby won for himself elevation to the peerage. At first Lord Wolseley had been asked simply to draw up the plans of the expedition; but as General Stephenson, the commander of the forces in Egypt, had not approved the scheme, Wolseley was called upon to assume the command himself. At his suggestion the government had decided upon the Nile route in opposition to the very generally expressed advice of the most competent authorities, among whom was General Stephenson. The latter favored the route from Sûakim to Berber as the most direct and the shortest. If an advance of only ten miles a day were made, this journey could be accomplished within a month. The objections to this route were the lack of water, and the certainty that Osman Digna would dispute every inch of the way. They were formidable objections certainly, but not insuperable.

The route would have been far preferable to the one decided upon, on account of the great saving in time.

There was still another route than the one chosen that seems never to have been considered, although it has always been the beaten way from Cairo to Khartnm. It coincides with the route Wolseley preferred, except that instead of making the long journey through the horse-shoe bend of the Nile, south of Wady Halfa, where the river is impassable to large craft on account of the cataracts, it strikes off across the Nubian desert from Korosko to Abn Hamed, the points that represent the heel of the shoe. The desert journey is accomplished in about six days, the distance being two hundred and thirty miles, or somewhat less than the distance from Snakim to Berber. The route is not altogether pleasant, as the line of skeletons of men and beasts who have perished on the way testifies; but there is a well at the midway station, and a flying column could have carried enough water along with it. In spite, however, of the greater disadvantages of the circuitous route, Wolseley decided to stick to the river.

The commander arrived in Egypt on the 8th of September, and began to make elaborate and tedious preparations. His force was to consist of ten thousand men. To transport them he had determined to employ Canadian boatmen, and to use small boats similar to those he had used in a Canadian expedition which he had commanded on the Red River some years before. The boats and boatmen were not ready before the end of September, when more than a month of high water had already been lost. If the expedition had started in July, as originally suggested, even steamers of light draft might have been towed up the cataracts, which, it must be remembered, are nothing more than long stretches of whirlpools and eddies that scarcely roar or rush as they wind in and out and around the thousand and one rocky islets. After the middle of August, when the Nile began to fall, every day passed was a precious day lost.

An impulse was given to the work at the end of September. A voice from the desert was heard that had been stilled for months. It had all of its old ring. "I am awaiting the British forces," wrote Gordon, " in order to evacuate the Egyptian garrisons." His purpose had not changed since the day he started for the Sûdan. On the 29th of September, Mr. Power's journal of events in Khartûm, from the 1st of May to the end of July, was given in the London *Times*. It was a thrilling story. The indignation that the following extract aroused was intense :

Since the despatch which arrived the day before yesterday [July 29], all hope of relief by our government is at an end; so when our provisions, which we have at a stretch for two months, are eaten, we must fall; nor is there any chance, with the soldiers we have, and the great crowd of women, children, *etc.*, of our being able to cut our way through the Arabs. We have not steamers for all, and it is only from the steamers we can meet the rebels.

The two months were past: had the garrison already fallen? Early in October further news was received contained in a series of dispatches sent by General Gordon to Massowah. None of them, however, bore a later date than Power's message to the *Times*. In one of them (July 31) Gordon writes:

Reading over your telegram of the 5th May, 1884, you ask me to state cause and intention in staying at Khartûm, knowing Government means to abandon Sûdan, and in answer I say, I stay at Khartûm because Arabs have shut us up, and will not let us out.

Again and again Gordon referred in his journal to the impertinence of the above request: State your reasons! "The '*reasons*' are those horribly plucky Arabs."[1]

The immediate result of these dispatches was that all eyes were turned upon Lord Wolseley. The criticism of his movements was less than the

[1] Journal, p. 53. (September 19.)

impatience at his delays. In the government's letter of instructions, dated October 8, he was informed that the primary object of his expedition was the rescue of General Gordon[1] and Colonel Stewart. He was not to go farther south than Dongola, unless it became actually necessary; and, in no case, was he to proceed beyond Khartûm, not even to relieve the garrison at Sennar. Such instructions were scarcely calculated to arouse Lord Wolseley to the activity that the purpose of his expedition required. Gordon had said that he could not leave Khartûm, and yet the government talked about rescuing him at a point midway between that city and Wady Halfa. The general who had stilled the cry of "Egypt for the Egyptians" with a skill and promptness that called forth the applause of the world, seemed to have assumed now a character quite in keeping with the desires of his government. They had been slow and irresolute in all their relations with the Sûdan. Each step was taken only when the irresistible force of public opinion compelled. By keeping just behind the public demand and the necessities of the moment, the government

[1] Gordon's view of the relief expedition is interesting in this connection. He wrote in his journals (September 24): " I altogether *decline* the imputation that the projected expedition has come to *relieve me*. It has *come to* SAVE OUR NATIONAL HONOR *in extricating the garrisons, etc., from a position in which our action in Egypt has placed these garrisons. I was relief expedition No* 1. *They are relief expedition No.* 2. . . . I am not the *rescued lamb*, and I will not be." The italics are his.

had acted always just too late. General Gordon gives a good instance of this failing in his journals:

> Take the Tokar business: had Baker been supported, say, by 500 men, he would not have been defeated; yet, after he was defeated, you go and send a force to relieve the town. Had Baker been supported by these 500 men, he would, in all probability, have been victorious, and would have pushed on to Berber; and, once there, Berber would not have fallen. What was right to do in *March*, was right to do in *February*. We sent an expedition in March, so we ought to have sent it in February; and then the worst of it was that, Baker having been defeated, *when you did send your expedition to Tokar*, Baker's force no longer existed, and his guns resist me at Berber. It is truly deplorable, the waste of men and money, on account of our indecision.[1]

The advance of the Nile force was lamentably slow. By the 20th of November there were only 3,000 troops, out of some 16,000 in Egypt, that had passed Wady Halfa. Within the next three weeks, however, the 10,000 troops composing the expeditionary force were all south of Korosko. It seemed as though Lord Wolseley were preparing to write a book on "My Winter on the Nile." He would have had the advantage of the thousand and one tourists who have written under the above title, in that he pushed beyond the usual limit at the first cataract, and maintained a progress that

[1] Gordon's Journals, p. 151. (October 8.)

all might envy, who have enjoyed the motionlessness of the dahabîeh. A description of a Nile journey is nothing unless it dwells upon the laziness, the idleness, the donothingness of the life.

In the meantime the news of another horror had been received from the Sûdan. On the 10th of September, General Gordon had sent Colonel Stewart down the Nile in command of an expedition against Berber. He considered it important that the rebel fortifications there should be destroyed, thus enabling Stewart to open communication with the expedition of relief, concerning whose movements Gordon was very much in the dark. It is also hinted that Gordon wished, by this method, to save the life of his brave lieutenant.[1] Before the fall of Berber he had sent down into Egypt more than six hundred soldiers and two thousand people; but this was the first attempt since then to add to the number. Stewart succeeded in demolishing the Berber fortifications, and then, with Power, the *Times* correspondent, and about forty others, he parted from the main force, which returned to Khartûm, and steamed on toward Dongola. After passing Abû Hamed—where he might have met a flying column from Korosko if that route had only been selected—his steamer struck a rock and could not be shoved off. He and his companions were

[1] A. Egmont Hake, The Story of Chinese Gordon, p. 180.

now induced by promises of peace to accept the hospitality of Suleiman Wad Gamr, in whose country they were. Unarmed, they met him at the house of a blind man to negotiate for the purchase of camels to take them to Dongola; but, while there, they were basely set upon and murdered. The bodies of Stewart and Power, the only Englishmen besides Gordon south of Dongola, were thrown into the river as food for the crocodiles. The valuable journals of Gordon and Stewart fell into the hands of the rebels. Hussein, the stoker of the steamer, escaped death, and after a servitude of four months gave the first authoritative report of the massacre. Undoubted rumors, however, had reached the force advancing up the Nile early in October. The news added fresh fuel to the fire of English indignation. The government that had shielded itself from the responsibility of Hicks's death could find no way of escape from the blame that now attached to it. Stewart had been appointed Gordon's first lieutenant, had been sent to the Sûdan for a specific purpose, and had then been abandoned to the fate that befell him. Those who had been wondering if the last act of the play were to be comedy or tragedy, questioned no longer. Alarming rumors were now circulated regarding Gordon. It was said that he had been captured by the Mahdi; then that Khartûm had fallen; and again that the mines had been exploded and had blown Gordon into the air. On the 14th of November, however, Wolseley received from Gordon a set of cipher dispatches, dated November 4. Gordon lived; but he was in imminent danger. The Mahdi was within eight hours of Khartûm, which had provisions for about forty days. Five steamers had gone from Khartûm to Metemneh to await the expected relief. These facts were kept from the public, which only knew that Gordon was alive.

The beginning of the new year found Lord Wolseley still working his tedious way up the Nile. The apathy that had followed long-continued impatience in England was dispelled, early in January, by a very explicit telegram from Lord Wolseley to the Prince of Wales. His lordship announced, with something of a theatrical air, that he would enter Khartûm on the 24th of January. The public confidence in Wolseley's promises was great; for he had always had a way of announcing what he proposed to accomplish on a certain day, and of proceeding forthwith to carry out his undertaking to the letter. Since the battle of Tel-el-Kebir, however, the public had been deluded by so many vain plans, never carried to their execution, that almost any promise must need go begging for confidence. Still the general public was willing to trust for a last time, and the recent article in the London *Times* was forgotten, that called upon Mr. Gladstone to resign "in order to enable a new ministry, not crippled by personal engagements injurious to the true interests of England, to adopt a vigorous policy in Egypt, the colonies, and foreign affairs generally."[1]

While Wolseley was hurrying his troops forward to Korti, which he had determined to make his base of operations, there were perplexing rumors afloat concerning the re-entrance of the Sublime Porte as an active factor in the Egyptian question. The announcement soon followed that the sultan was preparing to dispatch troops to Sûakim in order to overcome Osman Digna, who was still zealously serving the Mahdi in that locality. Her Majesty's government at once resolved that Turkish troops should not be landed on the Red Sea littoral. But on what ground could England prevent it? It had never claimed the power of a protectorate; how, then, could it exercise such power? The answer was easily found in the history of the preceding years. The British government had never hesitated to act as the dominant power; it had only hesitated to assume the responsibility that must necessarily be associated with that power. It seemed now as if England would be forced finally to acknowledge

[1] *The Times*, January 5, 1885.

herself the positive protector of Egypt, when suddenly the attention of the government and the people was diverted from diplomacy to the war operations in the Sûdan.

Having concentrated his forces at Korti, Lord Wolseley, on the 4th of January, ordered General Earle, with a force of about 2,500 men, to proceed to Berber, by way of the long bend in the Nile. He was to get possession of Abû Hamed and Berber, in order that the desert routes from those points might be made use of in case of evacuation. On the 8th of January, General Stewart, with a picked force of about 1,500 men, was dispatched from Korti straight across the desert to Metemneh, there to meet the steamers that General Gordon had sent out from Khartûm. This desert route was only about thirty miles shorter than the one from Korosko to Abû Hamed, which might have been taken in September. Four precious months would thus have been saved. All went well with General Stewart's desert journey, till he neared the wells of Abû Klea, less than twenty-five miles from Metemneh. He encamped near them on the 16th of January, and on the 17th his force was attacked by 10,000 rebels. His troops fought as Englishmen always fight; and the rebels, with all their superiority of numbers, were repulsed. The English loss was sixty-five killed and nearly a hundred wounded.

Among the former was the famous Colonel Burnaby, who made the wonderful "Ride to Khiva." He is said to have died "like a true British bull-dog, with his right hand clenched in death about the throat of the Arab whose spear was thrust through the Colonel's neck." On the 19th, a still more formidable force was encountered; but again the rebels were repulsed. General Stewart had received a wound which he would not admit was serious, but pushed on to Gûbat on the Nile, not attempting to force Metemneh, which was in the hands of the rebels. At Gûbat were Gordon's steamers and the inspiring message: 'All right at Khartûm. Can hold out for years." It seemed as if fortune served the will of England. The enthusiasm that greeted the news of Stewart's victories and of Gordon's message was boundless. A confidence was begotten that made final success seem already within England's grasp. The world did not know then, as we do now, that the message was written for the enemy,[1] and that Gordon had sent word to Wolseley, nearly two months before, that he had provisions enough for about forty days. The Commander-in-Chief had received a later dispatch, dated December 14, in which Gordon said: "Our troops in Khartûm are suffering from lack of provisions . . . We want you to come quickly." But Wolseley had

[1] A. Egmont Hake, Story of Chinese Gordon, p. 600.

kept Gordon's peril a secret, only using the utmost haste—at the eleventh hour—to secure his release. The world, therefore, rejoiced at the news.

Several days were now fatally misspent. It was not till the 24th of January that Sir Charles Wilson started on Gordon's steamers for Khartûm. On the 28th, after having been assailed all along his journey by armed Arabs on the banks of the river, Colonel Wilson appeared in sight of Khartûm. Instead of the eager welcome he expected, he was met with a furious fusilade from all sides, and before him on the government house floated the Mahdi's colors. Khartûm had fallen, and Gordon was captured or killed. Assured of the terrible disaster, Wilson hastily beat a retreat. He lost both his steamers at the sixth cataract, and only reached Gûbat after a most perilous adventure, being rescued from his dangerous situation by Lord Charles Beresford. But on the way down he had learned from the natives that Khartûm had fallen on the the 26th. Gordon had been lost by two days. With fateful instinct he had written, October 13: "It is, of course, on the cards that Khartûm is taken under the nose of the expeditionary force, which will be *just too late*."[1] It probably never will be known just how he died; and it matters little which story we believe. All agree that Faraz

[1] Journals, p. 178.

Pasha treacherously betrayed the city, and that the martyr died like a hero.

To the western world the news of the fall of Khartûm was like a thunderbolt from a clear sky. At the very moment of rejoicing, fortune and faith were crushed. The calamity marked an epoch. The press and the people demanded that from that day the great statesman, whose policy had always been peace, should bear the arms he was loath to assume and slow to use in a strong and swift campaign of revenge, or make way for a ministry of war. The public patience and forbearance were strained beyond their utmost tension. The final catastrophe was the natural outcome of all the mistakes of England in Egypt. Since the suppression of Arabi's rebellion there had been little to admire in the British policy. Forced to remain and protect her own interests, and guard with jealous care the water-way to India, England hesitated to accept, and endeavored to shirk at every step, the responsibility that her power and position had forced upon her. It may be true that the British interference in Egypt was not of Mr. Gladstone's choosing; but, when he accepted the control of the government, he accepted the situation in Egypt as it was, and not as he might wish it to be. Since his accession, in 1880, it had never been possible or desirable for England to withdraw her influence from Egypt;

but Mr. Gladstone could not look that fact in the face. After Arabi's downfall, in 1882, the British Parliament, press, and public urged their government to declare its policy or intentions in Egypt; but they urged in vain. Nothing was ever decided till the exigencies or the disasters of the moment rendered action absolutely imperative. This halting policy resulted in disaster, slaughter, and the final tragedy.

Scarcely had the world recovered from the first great shock of Gordon's death, when it was announced that General Earle had been killed in an engagement with the rebels, February 9, while pressing toward Abû Hamed; and then came the sad news that General Stewart's wound had proved fatal, February 16. Perhaps Wolseley began to have some concern for his own life. At all events, he lost no time in gathering together the outlying portions of his army. The perilous desert journey from Gûbat to Korti was safely made; and the river expedition that General Earle had commanded was recalled. With all possible expedition the army retreated to Dongola, where it took up its quarters for the summer. Such was the end of the lamentable failure to rescue Gordon.

The cry for vengeance with which England was still ringing had to be recognized in some way. To counteract the humiliation of Wolseley's retreat, active operations had been undertaken on the Red Sea littoral. Troops were personally reviewed by the queen, and then ordered to the seat of war in the eastern Sûdan. It was declared that the government had determined to open the route to Berber and then to "smash" the Mahdi. But the most barren, desolate, and difficult of desert routes was still guarded by Osman Digna, the lieutenant of the Mahdi, whose forces had more than once carried destruction into the English camp. It was a difficult task the government set the English soldiers, to accomplish that journey of two hundred and fifty miles amid all the natural perils of the desert and with hostile hordes ready to swoop down upon them from every mountain along the way. But the accomplishment was beyond the intention of the government. A show of activity was made at Snakim with soldiers and railway plant, until Mr. Gladstone had recovered from the effect of the vote of censure that so nearly [1] cost him his government when Parliament reassembled at the end of February. The beleaguered garrison of Kassala was sending piteous appeals for help that were like the old cries from Khartûm. But aside from this the call for war was still inspired of vengeance only. Vengeance, however, is a quality that Mr. Glad-

---

[1] The vote was carried in the upper House by a large majority, but lost in the lower House by the narrow majority of fourteen.

stone's character—to his honor be it said—has never known. Supported by a narrow majority, he turned his thoughts from the stinging failures of his policy abroad to the grand purposes of his life-work at home. The cry for vengeance never found an echo in the sand hills of the desert, while at home it had dwindled, within two months, to the murmur of a jeering and deriding opposition.

The epilogue of the tragedy, however, might better have been spoken after a farce. All the irony of an eighteenth century comedy was contained in Lord Wolseley's farewell address, in which he announced the withdrawal of the British troops from the Sûdan and highly praised "the conduct of all the departments of the service during the campaign." One asks to whom and to what he issued the farewell. Was it to the shades of Hicks Pasha, of the Stewarts, of Earle, of Gordon, and of the brave British soldiers whose whitening bones would make the desert paths plainer to the caravans of war or peace that should thereafter wind across the sands of the Sûdan? Or was it to the rival Mahdis—for since the death of Gordon the glory of Mehemet Ahmed had been dimmed by the claims of a Falser Prophet than himself — who were threatening a greater destruction among believers than had been accomplished by the trained troops of a superior civilization? Perhaps Osman Digna heard the address, or from the hills about Sûakim, where he and his band had so successfully harassed and hindered the invaders, watched the withdrawal. He must have smiled—for he was a European, and cannot be supposed to have acquired the disposition of the Mussulmans with their faith—as he looked down upon the few miles of the incomplete and deserted railway.

And yet the withdrawal from the Sûdan in May, 1885, was the wisest act of Mr. Gladstone's Sûdanese policy. Gordon himself had said: " If Khartûm falls, then go quietly back to Cairo, for you will only lose men and spend money uselessly in carrying on the campaign."[1] The troops could not go as far as Cairo, however, for the Egyptian boundary needed to be guarded. The frontier garrison was placed at Wady Halfa. This was the proper limit; for it brought Korosko, the terminus of the desert route, under the protection of the Nile patrol of steamers, and was itself within easy reach of reinforcements from Assûan. The natural barriers of protection, the long cataract south of Wady Halfa, and the six days' desert guarding Korosko, make the present Egyptian garrisons practically impregnable. And so the Sûdan was left to its inherent anarchy. But first England offered naïvely to let Turkey set up a government there. Turkey

[1] Journals, p. 179. (October 13.)

declined with thanks. The Sûdan pays no tribute. The Porte cares little for the mere honor of being acknowledged suzerain; its solicitude is for something more tangible. So long as there is no interference with her tribute prerogatives, Turkey will make no attempts to establish her claim of authority, by sending troops or treasure to Egypt or the Sûdan. After Turkey refused to act the part of what seemed cat's paw to England, Italy became clamorous for the distinction. But her ambition never has extended beyond the Red Sea littoral. The Sûdanese have thus been left practically to themselves since May, 1885. They have begun to prepare their country for the ultimate reception of civilization much more effectually than an external force could have done. The Mahdi and Osman Digna are dead. Intestine strifes among different factions have so wasted the resources of the land that the misery of the people is as great, probably, or greater than in the days when an Egyptian pasha was governor-general. Perhaps the people already look back upon the time when Gordon first ruled them, as the period of their happiest prosperity. It is not an impossibility that the dreams of Sir Samuel Baker may yet come true, in which he pictures to himself the upper Nile region as freed from the curse of the slave-traffic, as accessible to the outer world, and as bringing forth the bounties of tropical increase. Before this utopian result is secured, however, the influence of the Anglo-Saxon will again be needed.

We must now take a final look at Egypt proper. The khédive's government played a small part in the game that cost England so dearly. Their chief concern was to keep their head above the ever-flowing, never-ebbing tide of debts. It cannot be said that they succeeded. It has been seen to what extremities Lord Northbrook was obliged to go in order to relieve the financial embarrassments of 1884, and how the Powers were incensed at his action. By way of conciliation, a financial scheme was drawn up to which the Powers, in International Convention, agreed, and which was presented to Parliament in March, 1885. The agreement guaranteed a loan of £9,000,000, to be used in lifting the Egyptian debt, the loan to be liquidated by the repayment of £325,000 annually, and this sum to be considered the first charge against the Egyptian revenues until the entire loan is lifted. The administrative expenditure of the khédive's government was limited to the sum of £5,237,000. Any surplus over the year's receipts was to be paid over to the Commissioners of the Public Debt for the purpose of making good an imposed deduction of five per cent. from the interest on the loan and an imposed reduction of one-half per cent. from the interest on the Suez canal shares held by England. The customary provision was included in the agreement, that extends taxation to all foreigners resident in Egypt. This provision had often enough been endorsed; it must now be executed. The Egyptians would then believe that the Giaours were not without a sense of honor. The agreement further provided, as always, for an "exhaustive investigation into the revenue-earning capacity of Egypt." The final provision of importance was that if at the end of two years it should be found that a continued deduction from interest on the coupons is necessary, the khédive should summon an international commission like that of 1880, to make general inquiry into Egyptian finances. The agreement seemed to have been drawn up in the interest of Egypt.

The two years of probation are nearly ended. In the interval Egypt has prospered and the financial scheme has worked well. The Commissioners of the Public Debt now announce [1] that the surplus after the payment of the November coupon of the unified debt "will suffice to make good any deficiency in the unassigned revenues and to reimburse the five per cent. coupon tax levied during the last two years, besides leaving a balance, which under the convention will be equally divided between the *Caisse* and the Ministry of Finance." There will

[1] *The London Times*, October 26, 1886.

thus be no occasion for the khédive to summon an international commission. The comparative prosperity that has secured this result is due to the peaceful state of affairs in Egypt and to the more than ordinarily productive yield of the soil. The cotton crop has of late recalled the days when Ismail was khédive. Then, too, there has been a discovery within the boundaries of Egypt that may afford a better solution of the financial problem than all the agreements and investigations of European Powers can ever secure. Egypt has been absolutely unproductive of fuel; but there is a promise that the newly found petroleum will be made to answer the purpose of the imported coal. The new fuel has already been introduced by way of experiment on the Alexandria and Cairo railway.

There is one step remaining to be taken in Egypt that will do more than anything else toward securing the final settlement of the conflict between East and West. England must assume the burdens of her authority. She can never loose her hold of the country that guards the water-way to India. She is jealous of her power. When her attention was concentrated on the Afghan imbroglio in May, 1885, France thought it an opportune moment to regain her lost prestige in Egypt. But if England's attention was diverted for the moment, her representatives were not without power in Egypt. M. de

Freycinet failed as utterly then as he did in the day of Arabi. The complications that have arisen lately over the Bulgarian troubles have again pushed France to the front as the opponent of English domination in Egypt. Russia, of course, with her grasp upon Bulgaria and her eye ever on the Bosphorus, is inciting France to this opposition. The French press is filled with stories of the misrule that is prevalent in Egypt. But France will circulate stories reflecting on the policy of England in Egypt until she forgets the circumstances of her own retirement from responsibility. England has the single-handed control, and she means to maintain it. The welfare of Egypt rests on this resolution. Many people, who claim the divine right of judging the motives of an action and who fail to see so far as its results, urge that England is actuated solely by selfishness and the greed of power in asserting her control in Egypt, and that she is merely fortifying herself against that certain day when some protruding arm of Russian territory shall reach a southern sea. They say she makes the interest of Egypt secondary to her own ; therefore, the power of England in Egypt must be resisted. Granting even that these are England's motives, cannot the same wind blow good to both countries ? Is it a sound principle that what benefits one country must injure another ? The fact is, that the extension of the dominion of Great Britain, while bringing glory to the nation itself, is for the interest of the civilized world. The Anglo-Saxon influences of Christianity and civilization are the best known. As opposed to Russian influences they are both iconoclastic and creative. The Russian empire extends its dominion, and there appears no sign of assimilation; the subjugated people pays its tribute and its homage, but retains its language, its religion, and its customs. England, on the other hand, makes her furthermost territory British in reality as well as in name; ignorance, superstition, and savagery melt away under contact with the Anglo-Saxon influence. That England, in spite of all her mistakes, has had a beneficent influence upon Egypt, no one can doubt who compares the civilization under Mehemet Ali with that of to-day. This would be the trite assertion of an accepted fact, were it not for the stupendous financial follies of Ismail. The storm raged in his day; and the gloom still hangs over Egypt. It can only be swept away by the protecting arm of England. She has shrunk all along from the final step of annexation; but she remains the virtual suzerain of Egypt. A truly anomalous condition of affairs is presented to view. England has the control; Egypt bears the burdens; and Turkey reaps the profit. The rôle of Turkey is quite superfluous. She has never yielded to

Egypt the slightest return for the tribute she has regularly exacted and the troops she has occasionally employed. It is true that she granted Ismail the title of khédive for an enormous consideration; but if Mehemet Ali had been supported in his just struggle for independence in 1842, the ruler in Egypt might call himself khédive, emperor, or mikado, without the expenditure of a single piaster. It is not yet too late for severance. The vast sum of money paid by way of tribute to the Porte may be considered duly to have purchased for Egypt her independence of Turkey. This violation of contract could not be effected without a struggle. But with England's support it could result only in one way. Once accomplished, Egypt might yet shake off the shackles of debt, and the relations of the great Power of the West to Egypt in the East might be settled without conflict.

BOOKS AND PERIODICALS CONSULTED.

ABOUT, EDMOND. The Fellah.
ALLEN, CHARLES H., F.R.G.S. The Life of Chinese Gordon.
BAKER, Sir SAMUEL W. Ismailia.
BROADLEY, C. M. How We Defended Arabi.
DICEY, EDWARD. The Morning Land.
FORBES, ARCHIBALD. Chinese Gordon. Succinct Record of his Life.
GOODRICH, Lieutenant-Commander CASPER F. (U. S. Navy.) Report of the British Naval and Military Operations in Egypt, 1882.
GORDON, General C. G. Journals at Khartûm.
GRANT, ROBERT. History of the East India Company
HAKE, A. EGMONT. The Story of Chinese Gordon.
JERROLD, BLANCHARD. Egypt under Ismail Pasha.
—— The Belgium of the East.
KEAY, J. SEYMOUR. Spoiling the Egyptians. A Tale of Shame told from the British Blue Books.
LEON, EDWARD DE. The Khédive's Egypt.
LESSEPS, FERDINAND DE. The Suez Canal. Letters and Documents Descriptive of its Rise and Progress, 1854 to 1856.
LONG, Colonel C. CHAILLÉ. The Three Prophets : Chinese Gordon, Mehemet Ahmed, Arabi Pasha.
LORING, W. W. A Confederate Soldier in Egypt.
MCCARTHY, JUSTIN II., M.P. England under Gladstone, 1880–1885.
MCCOAN, J. C. Egypt As It Is.
PATTON, A. A., F.R.G.S. A History of the Egyptian Revolution to the Death of Mehemet Ali.
PEPPER, J. H. The Suez Canal. Published in Routledge's Discoveries and Inventions of the Nineteenth Century.
STONE, FANNY. Diary of an American Girl in Cairo during the War of 1882. *The Century*, June, 1884.
STONE, WILLIAM, M.A., F.L.S. Shall We Annex Egypt?

TOWLE, GEORGE MAKEPEACE.   England in Egypt.
WALLACE, D. MACKENZIE.   Egypt and the Egyptian Question.
WILSON, C. T., and FELKIN, R. W.   Uganda and the Egyptian Sûdan.
YATES, WILLIAM HOLT, M.D.   The Modern History and Condition of Egypt, 1801 to 1843.
Anonymous.   Egypt for the Egyptians : a Retrospect and a Prospect.
—— Plain Words on the Egyptian Question.

Appleton's Annual Cyclopædia has been of use, and files of the following journals have been consulted :

The British Quarterly Review.
The Contemporary Review.
The Edinburgh Review.
The Fortnightly Review.

The Independent.
The London Times.
The Nineteenth Century.
The Quarterly Review.

www.ingramcontent.com/pod-product-compliance
Lightning Source LLC
Chambersburg PA
CBHW020900230426
43666CB00008B/1248